NEW ENGLAND CHURCHES AND MEETINGHOUSES

NEW ENGLAND
CHURCHES & MEETINGHOUSES
1680-1830

Peter T. Mallary
Photographs by Tim Imrie

CHARTWELL
BOOKS, INC.

For RWB and GRM
Scholars and Friends

Published by
CHARTWELL BOOKS, INC.
A Division of BOOK SALES, INC.
110 Enterprise Avenue
Secaucus, New Jersey 07094

This book was designed and produced by
John Calmann and King Ltd, London
Designer: Richard Foenander

Text © 1985 John Calmann and King Ltd
Photographs © 1985 Tim Imrie

ISBN 9 89009 949 0

Filmset in Great Britain by Tradespools Ltd,
Frome, Somerset
Printed in Hong Kong by Mandarin Offset Ltd

INTRODUCTION

I
GOD AND MAN
IN NEW ENGLAND

1620-1700

Bartholomew Gosnold, Matthew Pring, Henry Hudson, Samuel de Champlain and John Smith were among the early explorers who first viewed the New England shoreline. Gosnold actually established a small colony on the Elizabeth Islands for a few weeks in 1602 and returned favorable reports of the rugged coast to England. Champlain wandered the shoreline and mapped Gloucester harbor, but eventually decided that his French settlement should be to the north, at Quebec. John Smith was the first Englishman to explore the New

1,2 Old St Paul's, Wickford, Rhode Island (1707): exterior and interior views.

England coast, in 1614, and gave the region its name. It is remarkable to think that just six years after Smith's investigation the Pilgrims arrived on that same coast, determined to remain. The *Mayflower* wanderers, though holding title to land in Virginia, found themselves in New England.

In the fall of 1620 the New England prospect for these exhausted travellers was fairly grim. Though the first winter the settlers endured was a moderate one by New England standards, it still presented difficulties for which most of these Pilgrims were unprepared. The nine-week crossing from England had weakened the voyagers; illness and the winter cold killed half the original band of one hundred by spring. William Bradford was the acknowledged leader of the settlers and served as Governor of their Plymouth colony during most of the years from their arrival until his death in 1657. His *History of the Plymouth Plantation*, not published until 1856, is invaluable, and provides us with a unique vision of the New England the Pilgrims found:

> But hear I cannot but stay and make a pause, and stand half amased at this poore peoples presente condition; and so I thinke will the reader too, when he well considers ye same. Being thus passed ye vast ocean, and a sea of troubles before in their preparation (as may be remembered by yt which wente before), they had now no friends to wellcome them, nor inns to entertaine or refresh their weatherbeaten bodys, no houses or much less townes to repaire too, to seeke for succoure. It is recorded in scripture as a mercie to ye apostle & his shipwraked company, yt the barbarians shewed them no smale kindness in refreshing them, but these savage barbarians, when they mette with them (as after will appeare) were readier to fill their sids full of arrows then otherwise. And for ye season it was winter, and they that know ye winters of yt countrie know them to be sharp & violent, & subjecte to cruell & feirce stormes, deangerous to travill to known places, much more to serch an unknown coast. Besids, what could they see but a hidious & desolate wilderness, full of wild beasts & wild men? and what multitudes ther might be of them they knew not. Netheir could they, as it were, goe up to ye tope of Pisgah, to vew from this wilderness a more goodly countrie to feed their hops; for which way soever they turnd their eys (save upward to ye heavens) they could have little solace or content in respecte of any outward objects. For summer being done, all things stand upon them with a wetherbeaten face; and ye whole countrie, full of woods & thickets, represented a wild & savage heiw. If they looked behind them, ther was ye mighty ocean which they had passed, and was now as a maine barr & goulfe to separate them from all ye civill parts of ye world.

It was an inauspicious beginning for this small settlement. The critical importance of this cold commencement is summed up simply by the nineteenth-century American historian George Bancroft, who called it "the origin of New England; it was the planting of the New England institutions."

3 Map of New England showing locations of churches and meetinghouses; and a view of Boston in 1848.

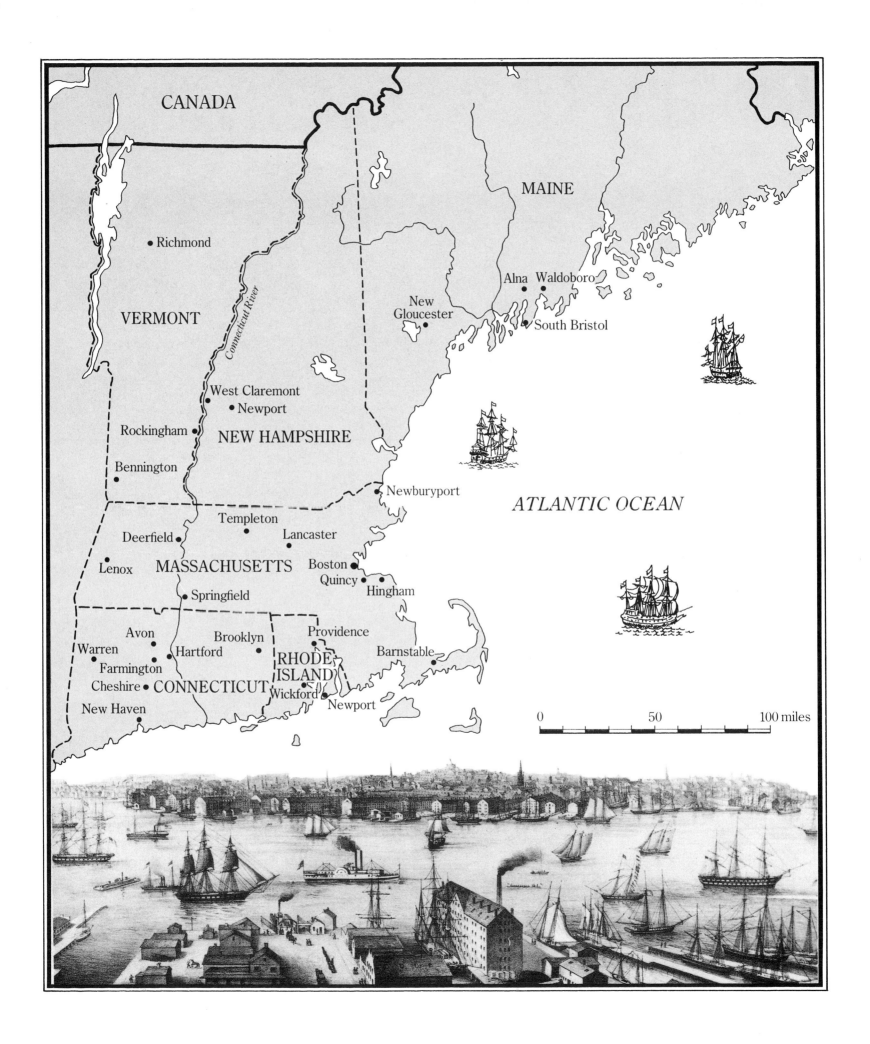

CANADA

MAINE

VERMONT

• Richmond

Alna • Waldoboro

New
Gloucester

• South Bristol

Connecticut River

West Claremont
• Newport

Rockingham •   NEW HAMPSHIRE

Bennington •

ATLANTIC OCEAN

• Newburyport

Templeton
Deerfield •   • Lancaster

Lenox •   MASSACHUSETTS   Boston •
Quincy •

Springfield •   Hingham

Avon •   Brooklyn   Providence •
Warren •   Hartford •   Barnstable •
Farmington •   RHODE
Cheshire •   CONNECTICUT   ISLAND
Wickford •
New Haven •   Newport

0   50   100 miles

The Pilgrims were a political and religious splinter group in the truest sense, dogmatic separatists from the established Church of England. They rejected the concerns of the physical world and strove instead for a humbleness and a piety which would ensure them a place in the spiritual world. They lacked the practical ability to expand the community they had founded beyond the borders established during their first decade although, while their business skills may have been limited, their honesty was impeccable. Long after the European investors in the Plymouth settlement had given up hope of recouping their money, the community continued to send whatever it could raise until the debt was finally paid. The highminded idealistic piety of the Pilgrims has become a staple of the American story. Eager descendants trace their lineage back to the *Mayflower* travellers. However, it was the Puritans, who settled at Massachusetts Bay, who changed the face of New England. The Pilgrims' utopian vision was probably their undoing. Meanwhile the Puritans were using similar religious and intellectual assumptions to more practical ends. They were shrewd at sums, and successfully filled the mercantile vacuum left by their Plymouth neighbors. The Puritans' energy took them up and down the New England coast, and into the interior.

The Puritan emigration of the 1630s was initially inspired by the creation of the Massachusetts Bay Company in 1628. The Company was formed by a group of prominent English Puritans interested in investment and settlement in New England and a charter was obtained in 1629 from Charles I. The founders of the Company included Sir Richard Saltonstall, Thomas Dudley and John Winthrop. John Endecott was the first Governor of the Bay Colony, from 1628 to 1630, arriving at Naumkeag (Salem). New Puritan settlements followed in a rush. Endecott went to Mishawum (Charlestown) while others settled such places as Shawmut (Boston), Mystic (Medford), Watertown, Roxbury, Dorchester, Dedham and Concord. In 1633, King Charles appointed the energetically anti-Puritan Bishop of London, William Laud, Archbishop of Canterbury, and therefore head of the established English Church. This did much to spur emigration of Puritan dissenters, and by the 1640s 20,000 souls had come to New England. During this crucial decade, Connecticut was opened up because of the relentless search for new land. Chief among these southwestern colonizations were Hartford, founded by Thomas Hooker in 1636, and New Haven, founded by John Davenport and Theophilus Eaton.

The charter for the Massachusettts Bay Company had inadvertently established an entity which could function with remarkable independence. John Winthrop, newly arrived as Governor in 1630, swiftly established the Company's civil authority in the form of a General Court with freemen representation from all the settlements. Freemanship was limited to company stockholders, and the franchise, though it was extended as early as 1661, was initially limited to church members. This civil body enjoyed real, if not wholly democratic, power. The General Court model was followed by other more distant groups of communities such as the New Haven Colony, which established its own court system in 1639. As early as 1644 the General Court in Massachusetts had developed into a legislative body with two houses, the Deputies (or executives) and the Assistants (or advisors). Elections were held annually.

4 The Old Ship Meetinghouse, Hingham, Massachusetts (1681):
a 19th-century view.

5 Second Church, Hartford,
Connecticut (1826):
a 19th-century view.

The General Court played an important role in the expansion and settlement of New England, because it authorized grants of land to members of a parish wishing to establish an independent community. The original petitioners to the Court became the new town's proprietors, usually receiving a grant about six miles square. New towns were generally designed eventually to house sixty to eighty families. The proprietors laid out the land with this in mind. First they would select a spot for the central village, often chosen with frontier defense in mind. Town roads would shoot off from this central point, which usually had a common and the town's meetinghouse. Originally the common was exactly what its name implies, being used for community cultivation or pasture. In the earliest communities the meetinghouses also served as garrisons. House lots would be apportioned near the common or green. These lots consisted of about five to ten acres, and were laid out in an attempt to maintain equal values. The lots were distributed by drawing numbers from a hat, though some were always set aside for a meetinghouse, a minister, a school, and for later arrivals. Farmland surrounding the village was laid out and distributed in a similar fashion. In some communities the proprietors with the most to bring to the new settlement received more land; in others, the reverse was true. This form of distribution led to awkward patchworks of farm property holdings, which were often simplified by swapping lots. This system for setting up a new town became the New England standard.

It would be easy to stop here and paint, or even print, a charming picture of one of these lovely New England village greens. Certainly there are few things more blissfully bucolic. Places like Strafford, Vermont, with its meetinghouse towering above the green, retain the pristine Currier & Ives quality most people associate with the pleasure of rural life. As we have already seen, however, life on New England's shores and hillsides was not always so peaceful. The weather was cold, the growing season was short, and relations between the invaders and the invaded were not always cordial.

It is impossible to understand the settlers, their dwelling-places, or their meetinghouses without reckoning with their hearts and minds and, inevitably, their God. Religion, rather than excessive moralism or materialism, was the seventeenth-century Puritan's guiding force. Their flight to the New England wilderness was inspired by their vision of divine providence. From Maine to the Connecticut River Valley it was God who illuminated their steps or, as the eminent Massachusetts Puritan Cotton Mather put it, "His Divine Providence hath irradiated an Indian Wilderness."

Though the General Court may have granted lands and settled certain civil disputes in these fledgling settlements, the main influence on community life was God's word as delivered from the pulpit. The New England Puritans' certain application of God's will, so easily chuckled at today, was vital in ordering an as yet unshaped society, in an often hostile environment. One reason the word "church" was difficult for early New Englanders, other than its obvious Papist overtones, was that it was not sufficiently encompassing. Puritan religion was a way of life, not simply a building or even a congregation. This lifestyle, which came to be commonly known as the New England Way, gave birth to the idea of congregationalism. According to the historian Daniel Boorstin:

> The basic fact about congregationalism was its emphasis on the going relationship among men. Each church was not part of a hierarchy, or a branch of a perfected institution, but a kind of club composed of individual Christians searching for a godly way of life . . . At the heart of the congregational idea was the unifying notion that a proper Christian church was one adapted to the special circumstances of its place and arising out of the continuing agreement of certain particular Christians.

Periodic synods which gathered New England's most prominent church leaders provided whatever slim, centralized government the early church required or desired. The Cambridge Platform, annunciated at such a synod in 1648 at Cambridge, Massachusetts, produced a stated basis for these independent parishes. It disdained episcopacy and endorsed congregational individuality. The reasons were both practical, brought about by the realities of distance and difficult communication, and doctrinal—the New England Puritan divines claimed to repudiate the contentiousness of European church government. They did, however, maintain their ties with the Church of England by stating a "desire to hold forth the same doctrine (especially in fundamentalls [*sic*]) which wee see & know to be the churches of England, according to the truth of the Gospell [*sic*]."

Two things were emblematic of the Word in these frontier communities: the meetinghouse and, standing in its pulpit, the divine. The meetinghouse was the center for activities both secular and theological; and the pulpit, not the altar, was the centerpiece of the meetinghouse. In terms of civil authority the power of the minister was somewhat limited. He was usually unable to hold public office and was, at least in theory, answerable to the will of his congregation. His power came from the pulpit. The minister's word was the absolute delineation of the New England Way. While the meetinghouse was the structure for the delivery of the Word, the sermon gave the Word a unique New England form.

Attendance at meeting was compulsory, but most members went along gladly, as the meetings were the intellectual and social high spot of the week. There were two sermons on Sunday, with a break for socializing and gossip in between, and there was often a Thursday meeting as well. There are many stories of efforts to rouse weary listeners during these two-hour sessions, but more often attentive members brought notebooks so as to lead family discussion later in the week. The sermons had a standard form. They began with a textual reference, continued with a discussion of that text, and concluded, most importantly, with an illumination of its application to daily life. These instructions were usually firm, and sometimes sound strange to modern ears, but there was not much room for spiritual question-marks in these struggling settlements.

The modern reader may hear nothing but sometimes biting rhetoric in the words of Puritan divines such as John Cotton, Thomas Hooker, Increase and Cotton Mather or, later, Jonathan Edwards. But there was light and vision too. A fine summing up of the Puritan image comes from Hooker:

> So I would have you do, loose your selves, and all ordinances, and all that you
> have, and do, in the Lord Christ . . . Let all bee swallowed up, and let nothing
> be seene but a Christ . . . As it is with the Moone and Starres, when the Sunne
> comes, they loose all their light, though they are in the heavens still; and as it is
> with rivers, they all goe into the sea, and are swallowed up of the Sea . . . So let
> it be with thy Soule, when thou wouldest finde mercy and grace.

Edwards, the most universally known of New England's Puritan preachers, belongs chronologically to the next section, as he wrote one hundred years after Hooker. The Enfield sermon, "Sinners in the Hands of an Angry God", is probably Edwards's most famous, but this vituperative oration is also one of his least representative works. Here are some posthumously published words from his *Dissertation Concerning the End for Which God Created the World* (1765), which are aptly placed here next to Hooker's:

> The great and last end of God's words . . . is indeed but *one*; and this *one* end is
> most comprehensively called, THE GLORY OF GOD . . . and is fitly compared
> to an effulgence or emanation of light from a luminary. . . . Light is the external
> expression, exhibition and manifestation of the excellency of the luminary, of the
> sun for instance. . . . It is by this that all nature is quickened and received life,

comfort and joy. . . . The emanation or communication of the divine joy in God, has relation indeed both to God, and the creature; but it has relation to God as its fountain, and as the beams of the sun are something of the sun . . . In the creatures knowing, esteeming, loving, rejoicing in, and praising God, the glory of God is both exhibited and acknowledged; his fullness is received and returned. Here is both an *emanation* and a *reemanation*. The refulgence shines upon and into the creature, and is reflected back to the luminary. The beams of glory come from God, and are something of God, and are refunede back again to their original. So that the whole is *of* God, and *in* God, and *to* God, and God is the beginning, middle and end in this affair.

These Puritan preachers may have been rigid in their instruction and consequently harsh in their judgments, but they also understood that cold winters must sometimes be combatted with a Godly vision of spiritual light and warmth. Particularly during the first two colonial generations they served as the compasses for their communities.

A critical factor in the development of Puritanism was the generally held feeling that the separation of the English from the Roman Catholic Church had been superficial, a "divorce of

6 Newport, New Hampshire, with the meetinghouse of 1822 on the right: a 19th-century view.

convenience." A number of doctrinal differences stemmed from this; membership is an important example. The Anglicans rejected the notion that one of their functions was the administration of a litmus test to establish its brethrens' earthly state of grace and therefore a person's right to membership. The Church was to serve as a framework for God's work on earth and a bridge to His heavenly kingdom, but all Christians were welcome. The Puritan standard was far more rigid. A prerequisite to membership in a New England congregation was the earthly demonstration of the state of grace, a conversion attested to before the meeting. This, to the Puritan mind, ensured that their gatherings would be a true communion of "visible saints." The Presbyterians, dramatically outnumbered in New England by their Congregational counterparts, found a slightly different route by entrusting their leadership to an "elect." Puritan dominance made membership a critical rite of passage in most New England communities.

This stand was not a serious problem for the first generation. They would not have ventured across the Atlantic if their position within the Puritan framework had not been quite certain. As the seventeenth century wore on, however, the issue became more complicated. The question of whether membership should be automatically extended to the children of "visible saints" became critical.

A Massachusetts synod of 1662 arrived at a controversial compromise called the Half-Way Covenant. The Covenant granted church membership to the children of first-generation Congregationalists, but denied them participation in the Lord's Supper until more demonstrable evidence of conversion was forthcoming. This solution was a classic piece of Puritan practicality. It kept the meetinghouse benches filled and assured the orderly transfer of community leadership, while retaining the purity of the sacrament. Solomon Stoddard of Northampton, the leading liberal opponent of the Covenant, deemed the Lord's Supper a "converting ordinance" and extended it to all. Stoddard's approach was widely accepted in the Connecticut Valley and elsewhere in that colony. (His liberal legacy was destined both to inspire and to haunt the career of his grandson, Jonathan Edwards.)

New England's seventeenth-century Puritans have been energetically lampooned as prudish, prohibitionist, fundamentalist, intolerant, bigoted, fanatic, overly superstitious, cruel in judicial proceedings, theocrats, power-hungry and economically motivated, moralistic, humorless and as hating art. The final two attributes are largely true. The dry Yankee wit we associate with New England is largely a post-Puritan development. Art was often viewed as detracting from, rather than, as in so many other religious traditions, enhancing, Man's vision of God.

Some of the other accusations are downright incorrect, such as that they were fundamentalists. The Puritans certainly believed the Bible to be the Word of God, and felt that every syllable required careful attention, but they also accepted that the Word required reasonable interpretation. Though they were scriptural in their approach, they were not literalists. Again, the Puritans were neither particularly prudish nor prohibitionist. Some records show ministers chastising male parishioners in open meeting for lack of sexual attention to their wives. As far as liquor was concerned, tippling was accepted, drunkenness

7 After meeting in Lancaster, Massachusetts, *c.*1900.

8 The town green at Lancaster, Massachusetts, with its fine Bulfinch meetinghouse on the left: a 19th-century view.

abhorred. The Puritans certainly embraced a strict moral code. The restrictive bluelaws are often held up as a good example of New England repression in action. However, the most absurd of these laws were the deliberate invention of Samuel Peters, an Anglican minister from Connecticut, in his anti-Puritan *General History of Connecticut* (1781). Massachusetts Bay is often assumed to have been governed religiously. However, although its ministers were among its leading and most influential citizens, and the relationship between church and state was one of the central issues of its early generations, it was no more a theocracy than the mother country. The colony was governed by the General Court.

The other stereotypes are misleading unless placed in context. Puritan criminal justice in New England was generally on a par with, or even ahead of, its European counterparts. Some punishments may seem bizarre or cruel by modern standards, but many tools of torture which were common in parts of Europe were never applied in New England, and capital punishment, though always cause for a sermon and a spectacle, was rarer than in England. Though the Salem witch-trials of the 1690s are world-renowned, bouts with superstition and the occasional witchhunt in New England were no more common than in the mother country. The issue of religious toleration and bigotry is a complicated one. Before 1660 Massachusetts was probably more tolerant than England, New York, or Virginia, the seat of the Anglican Church in America; but during the late seventeenth century it was less so. Generally, the Puritan methods of protecting their religious purity were in line with their times. European Puritans were dissenters by definition and they were fond of sectarian and doctrinal feuding. In New England, the Puritan Way was tantamount to the Established Way, and dissent, particularly during the first two generations, was viewed as a serious threat. Ironically, the banishment of some dissenters led to the establishment of Rhode Island, arguably the most tolerant place in the seventeenth-century world. The stories of dissenters such as Anne Hutchinson and Roger Williams shed much light on Puritan justice in New England.

Williams's confrontation is the better known of the two. He arrived in New England an unrepentant separatist, whose views were instantly too radical for the Puritans. He enjoyed a brief tenure as minister at Salem, but his pronouncements soon put him on a collision course with the General Court. Though his liberal views on religious toleration set him at odds with the divines, it was conflict over secular issues which finally led to his banishment. Williams stated that the Massachusetts Bay charter was illegal because it abrogated Indian rights, and that civil authority had no reasonable jurisdiction in matters of conscience. His exile became inevitable, and in 1635 he left for Rhode Island. Williams's Providence Plantations became the seat of New England toleration. He welcomed the establishment of the American Baptist Church, and admitted Quakers and Jews. His printed bouts with John Cotton, who saw the roles of church and state as inextricably interwoven, are seminal in American intellectual history.

Anne Hutchinson's case is equally revealing. She incurred the wrath of the establishment through her weekly meetings to discuss recent sermons. She saw the Puritan establishment, not entirely incorrectly, as too concerned with the worldly manifestations of religion, and not sufficiently imbued with the energetic spirituality she embraced. She felt that faith alone met the requirements for salvation. She was a charismatic figure and gathered around her enough supporters to command the attention of the Court. They accused her, also with some justification, of social disruption.

Her trial in 1637 was dramatic. The Court heard reams of testimony, both civil and theological, which attempted to delineate her crimes and heresies. Much has been made of reported cruelty to Hutchinson during the trial, but it is probable that there was no particular excess and, other than its notoriety, her trial was little different from others. There is no doubt that her defense was adroit and articulate. As the trial drew to a close it appeared very likely that she might win. With a characteristic sense of the dramatic, at this point she sealed her own fate, announcing to the assembled multitude that her understanding of the Way was based on direct communication with the Almighty. Her inevitable conviction did not result in her being flogged, burned, hanged or even pilloried—her fame was probably of some assistance in this regard. Like Williams she was banished but, because it was winter and she was pregnant, her dismissal was postponed until spring. She then received a further hearing and after first agreeing, and then refusing, to recant, she followed Williams to Rhode Island. The cases of Williams and Hutchinson both represent important early departures from the New England Way; their dissention could only be dealt with by removing them from the Puritan mainstream.

This book emphasizes the religious experience of the white men who displaced the American Indian on the shores of New England. Roger Williams's statements show that there was some uncertainty among dissenters about the justification of this displacement. Most of the Puritan brethren, however, were confident that their vision would bring salvation to Cotton Mather's "Indian Wilderness." John Eliot founded the Society for the Propagation of the Gospel in New England (not the later Anglican SPG) to facilitate the establishment of his communities of converted or "praying" Indians. It is clear that the Puritans saw their role as saviours from the first. Though their approach ranged from condescension and arrogance to occasional confrontation, this attitude was based on a practical and often benevolent, albeit very European, set of assumptions. The Massachusetts Bay charter called for "the conversion of such savages as yet remain wandering in desolation." Nothing states more clearly the certainty of the Puritan vision than the depiction on the colonial seal of an American Indian imploring his European neighbor to "Come Over and Help Us." White men and red men were doomed to collision from the moment of the *Mayflower*'s first landfall. While one cannot fail to see the validity of Roger Williams's position, one can also understand the inevitability of Puritan priorities and conclusions.

II
PURITANS BECOME YANKEES
1700-1800

The end of the seventeenth century saw the New England Way, if not in disarray, at least somewhat disheveled. The heart of seventeenth-century life had been the Word. The eighteenth saw earthly pursuits demand equal status with spiritual clarity. In his excellent study of Connecticut society between 1690 and 1765, *From Puritan to Yankee*, Richard Bushman states:

> After 1690 the people outgrew the towns, and interests in lands and trade
> beyond the borders engaged men in enterprises over which the meeting had no
> control. . . . Until 1740, at least, no one in Connecticut recognized that the old
> concepts were outmoded. . . . A change in men's hearts had brought a general
> deterioration. People loved wealth more than religion.

The Rev. Mr Jonathan Marsh said in a 1721 sermon in Hartford that the issue was "our changing our God, our Glory, for the creature that can't satisfy us or make us happy people." The New England world was no longer a tentative series of settlements, fueled by religious conviction and struggling for survival. The frontier was very real, but the inexorable march west had already begun. There was no question of abandoning New England's shores. With this change came confidence, which bred material success, and which in turn led to a changing role for New England's Congregationalists. People were not all as convinced as the Rev. Marsh that earthly rewards would make them miserable. Cotton Mather summed up the older orthodox view:

> Religion brought forth prosperity, and the daughter destroyed the mother . . .
> There is danger lest the enchantments of this world make them forget their
> errand in the wilderness.

The "thrifty", but successful, Yankee was on his way.

Increase and Cotton Mather, father and son and two of the most important Puritan voices of the seventeenth century, continued as leaders of Congregational orthodoxy in the early eighteenth century. In the late 1680s and the early 1690s Increase played a central role in the renewal of the Massachusetts charter which, in the retention of its liberal aspects, continued to sow some of the earliest seeds of independent American thought. Father and son differed on the issue of the Salem witch-trials though they both opposed the executions. In 1702 Cotton published his *Magnalia Christi Americana*, the masterpiece of Puritan ecclesiastical history, but in 1703 he resigned as a Harvard fellow because the university's strict Congregational polity was in flux. The uncertainty and liberal religious leanings which Cotton observed at Harvard were symptomatic of the changing New England scene. Though Increase eventually supported the Half-Way Covenant, some of its effects must have distressed him. Though the meetinghouses were usually full the half-way membership made many a member's trip to meeting largely a formality. This may be an accepted state of affairs for the twentieth-century minister, but it was anathema to the orthodox Puritan divine.

Ever since Thomas Hooker and John Davenport had founded Hartford and New Haven in the 1630s, Connecticut and its River Valley settlements had established subtle but definite differences from its Massachusetts parent. In 1706, at the urging of Connecticut Governor Saltonstall, the clergy adopted a new platform for church discipline at Saybrook. Its most dramatic departure from the Cambridge Platform was to question the absolute independence of individual congregations. The Saybrook Platform established a group of county councils or consociations which were made up of clergy and lay delegates. In a period of waning religious fervor this associative structure, more presbyterian in nature, greatly increased the clergy's power. A minister now had the unified strength of the entire consociation for support when dealing with dissent. This new church structure moved Connecticut even further from the Massachusetts parent and closer to New York's Presbyterians. In fact, in parts of Connecticut the terms Congregational and Presbyterian became almost interchangeable.

Acceptance of the new Platform was not universal. New Haven dragged its feet, and various prominent leaders voiced their dissatisfaction. One of these, Roger Wolcott, wrote a refutation as late as the 1730s in which he suggested that the consociation structure vested the same power in the councils which the King had in the Church of England or (heaven forfend) the Pope had in the Roman Church. Wolcott was quick to state that it wasn't that he didn't trust the clergy, but that "it is not safe to trust the whole power of order in their hands." This was, in fact, a moderate expression of a feeling which was suddenly surprisingly widespread. The clergy, whose leadership had been unquestioned during much of the previous century, were now viewed by many as anything from ineffectual to untrustworthy. Another indication of Congregational unrest was the defection of the leading Puritan lights at Yale to the Church of England in 1722.

Northampton, Massachusetts, north of Hartford in the Connecticut River Valley, had long been a hotbed of religious upheaval. Solomon Stoddard, the longtime minister there, had liberally extended the Half-Way Covenant. This position had fostered five distinct periods of religious awakening in the area. Stoddard's ministry was one of the most active and one of the most controversial in New England. His ties were more with Connecticut than with eastern Massachusetts. The Saybrook Platform was energetically endorsed by Stoddard, and he encouraged the formation of consociations from Deerfield to the Connecticut shore. Three years before his death in 1727 Stoddard's grandson, Jonathan Edwards, came to assist at the Northampton parish. The drift away from orthodox Puritanism during the first half of

9 First or Center Church, Hartford, Connecticut (1806).

the eighteenth century provided fertile territory for religious revivalism. Edwards, partly through the rejection of his grandfather's liberal policies, was poised to become the movement's initial spokesman.

Jonathan Edwards was born in East Windsor, Connecticut, the son of that community's minister. By the time he reached Northampton he had graduated from Yale and had preached and taught there. His approach to his ministry was that of the consummate intellectual. Edwards devoted thirteen hours a day to his studies and sermon writing, producing two a week. He was not particularly interested in the pastoral ministry. Rather, in the spirit of many of his seventeenth-century forebears, he believed that his pulpit orations were of paramount importance. His wife, Sarah Pierpoint, took up many of the more personal tasks of his ministry, and her remarkable efforts made their home the gathering place for many members of the community. The American schoolboy's image of Edwards raining terror from his pulpit is absurd. His delivery was in fact restrained; not loud, but distinct. Edwards let his words roar for him.

Edwards derived more from his seventeenth-century predecessors than his sermon-writing habits. He also embraced the more stringent conservative philosophy of his Puritan forebears, and rejected the move away from their principles during the early years of the eighteenth century. He saw this drift as an inevitable step toward popery. In 1734 Edwards took to his pulpit to deliver a series of sermons which addressed these and related questions. His simple reawakening of the early Puritan vision brought about conversions and applications for church membership of a type, and at a rate, not seen since the Half-Way Covenant. It also caused some members, more used to Stoddardian liberality, to feel singled out. Edwards proclaimed his delight with the "glorious attention" paid to questions religious:

> Other discourse than of the things of religion would scarcely be tolerated in any
> company in the spring and summer following anno 1735, the town seemed to be
> full of the prescence of God: it was never so full of love, nor so full of joy, and
> yet so full of distress as it was then.

The Great Awakening blossomed. The revival spread gradually, and the groundwork was laid for the arrival in New England in 1740 of the greatest popular preacher of the eighteenth century, the Methodist George Whitefield. Whitefield's orations were greeted by overflow crowds. He brought his bombastic and impassioned style to gatherings as large as eight thousand in Boston. He delivered a series of sermons in Northampton which reduced Edwards to tears. Physical manifestations of conversion were commonplace and professions of conversion came in the hundreds. During the next year Edwards and other preachers of his stature took to the road as the fever of revival reached its crest. It was during this tour that Edwards delivered his immortal Enfield sermon. Its powerful message was greeted by so much weeping and shaking from the congregation that Edwards had to beg for quiet.

The Awakening was far from universally applauded. A group of New England ministers, led by Charles Chauncey of Boston, felt that the revival was a great regressive step. Chauncey outlined his thoughts in *Seasonable Thoughts on the State of Religion in New England* (1743). In an ironic but logical twist of language, Edwards's followers, who endorsed the old Puritan orthodoxy, were known as the "New Lights," while Chauncey's more progressive adherents were known as the "Old Lights." Many congregations were divided and the revivalists often withdrew, becoming known as separatists or "Separates."

These Separates had a profound effect on the emergence of denominationalism in New England. Though some New Light Separates formed their own congregations, many others were drawn to the Baptist Church, always a comparatively small sect, which had fallen into a particularly dispirited state. They welcomed the infusion of new membership. Doctrinally this move was not difficult as it was only a small leap of faith from the Puritan "visible saint" to the Baptist reservation of baptism for reborn adults. Likewise, the Anglican Church was invigorated by many disaffected Old Lights. Many prominent families, offended by New Light showmanship and tired of endless division and confusion within the Congregational parishes, sought refuge in the Church of England.

The Great Awakening was a bright, but brief, flame. By 1745, even at the site of its birth in Northampton, the revival was largely dead. Not a single new application for membership was made there from 1744 to 1748. Whitefield made a number of return visits and always attracted attention, but he was largely preaching to the converted. In 1750, probably in an attempt to rouse old passions, Edwards demanded the repeal of the Half-Way Covenant, but the Stoddard legacy died hard in Northampton and Edwards had gone too far. He was dismissed in 1750. His writings during the next eight years, however, were among his most important. The clarity of his thinking coupled with the gradual moderation of some of his views meant that he remained the primary exponent of conservative Congregational thought in New England. The religious geography was sharpened by the Awakening. While Connecticut and western Massachusetts (along the valley) embraced Edwards's modified conservatism, Boston and eastern Massachusetts became the center for liberal theology eventually spawning Unitarianism and Universalism.

The Great Awakening left New England's various churches and people still predominantly Congregational, but with more denominational variety than ever before. Richard Bushman suggests that the Awakening was an outlet for guilty sinners who had come to care more about earthly Yankee concerns and had surrendered less to their Puritan God. He further suggests that, far from slowing the drift from the old Puritan road, the individualist nature of the revival, combined with eighteenth-century commercial growth, may have

10,11 Christ Church, Boston, Massachusetts (1723): the choir in 1905, and a 19th-century view of the interior.

actually hastened the emergence of the New England Yankee. The Awakening bore no great spiritual fruit, and, in fact, the religious historian William Warren Sweet has referred to the next fifty years of New England's religious progress as years of "spiritual deadness."

This post-revival era may have been less spritually energetic, but it did not leave most of the ministers idle. During the years prior to the Revolution they became political activists. Half a century after the Revolution, the French observer Alexis de Tocqueville noted that American religion, "must be regarded as the foremost of political institutions. . . . I am certain that they hold it to be indispensable to the maintenance of republican institutions." His point seems particularly relevant to the role of New England's Congregationalists in the Revolution. The path along the New England Way was seen as one of liberation as surely as the course across the Atlantic was charted in search of religious liberty. The Great Awakening, which spread well beyond New England's boundaries, was the first great American experiment in politics. Rival factions emerged and intercolonial leaders appeared. In New England, the Anglican Church grew and the Congregationalists and Presbyterians banded together in opposition. By the middle of the eighteenth century the American colonies were arguably the most advanced Protestant community in the world. The standard of education was high and the works of Milton, Sidney and Locke were widely read and appreciated. All in all, it is not so surprising that by about 1750 the word "liberty" was approaching equal status with the word "salvation" in the New England pulpit.

In writing *Meetinghouse Hill* (1952) Ola Elizabeth Winslow combed hundreds of sermons to enliven her work. Locke's ideals of freedom and equality as a fundamental human right are certainly reflected in the examples I have borrowed:

> To speak of the opposite of liberty is to speak a Language unintelligible to the greater Part of the New-English people . . . we enjoy Liberty to as great Perfection, if not greater than any people besides on this earth. When I look over a numerous Assembly of New-English people, I can but bless God, and Congratulate my Country, at the sight of so many free People, who carry Liberty in their faces.
>
> *(Nathanael Hunn, 1747)*

> There is not a member of the Body politick to be despised; nor may one glory over another, as if he stood in no Relation to him, or had no Dependence upon him . . . we are all, even Rulers themselves, and Ministers of the Gospel, subject to the same Laws, as the common People; and we are all members of the same Commonwealth.
>
> *(Jonathan Ingersoll, New London, 1761)*

> We are called to Freedom and Liberty. Liberty! May we never know its worth and inestimable value by being strip't and depriv't of it.
>
> *(James Lockwood, 1759)*

When our liberty is invaded and struck at, 'tis sufficient Reason for our making war for the Defence or Recovery of it . . . To live is to be free,—Therefore when our Liberty is attacked, . . . 'tis time to rouze, and defend our undoubted and invaluable Priveleges, we fight for our Liberties, our Religion, our Lives.

(James Cogswell, 1757)

Two final quotations have a particularly fateful ring. The second is a rhetorical response to any attempts to invade New England's frontiers or to "enslave our free-born mind":

None of my present Audience will question whether the profession of a soldier is consistent with the character of a Christian.

(Ebenezer Pemberton, 1757)

Then the Sword is, as it were, consecrated to God, and the Art of War becomes a part of our Religion.

(Samuel Davies, 1758)

Certainly the word liberty was often used in conjunction with the phrase "rights of Englishmen," but by the 1750s and 1760s the connection was not always so clearly stated, and the notion of a common colonial interest began to emerge from the pulpit. As the crisis grew in the early 1770s the meetinghouse regained its central role in many New England villages. The townspeople, as a natural outgrowth of their simple democracies, used these buildings to hammer out statements on the issues in the conflict. In Ola Winslow's words, "month by month . . . towns, kept on acting, each in turn writing its own Declaration of Independence."

When the war came, the leaders of New England's Congregational communities stood at the head of a church militant, and their participation did not end at the pulpit. When David Avery at Gageboro, Massachusetts, heard the news from Lexington he presented a farewell sermon, gathered twenty recruits and proceeded to march, recruiting as he went. This scene was repeated throughout New England. The ministers served as fighters, recruiters, officers and chaplains. Many donated their salaries to the effort, often to buy powder for their town. James Lyons, minister at Machais, Maine, started a salt factory by distilling sea water. "Parson Lyons' Salt Factory" supplied the region for the entire war. He also refused his salary for three years.

The Presbyterians, still locked in alliance with the Congregationalists, were almost universally supportive of the Patriot position. The Baptists were also largely on the revolutionary side both because of their bitter feud with New England's Anglicans and because of their commitment to religious liberty infringed on by the Massachusetts' church. The Methodists, on the other hand, were mostly bound by the Tory stand of their leader, John Wesley. The arguments of American Anglican Samuel Johnson convinced Wesley to support the loyalist position.

The position of the Anglican Church in the colonies at the time of the Revolution is of

12 Trinity Church, Newport, Rhode Island (1725):
a 19th-century view.

13 First Church, Springfield, Massachusetts (1818):
a 19th-century view.

particular interest. The Anglicans produced two-thirds of the signers of the Declaration (six of them were the sons or grandsons of Anglican clergymen): George Washington, James Madison, Patrick Henry and Alexander Hamilton were all Church of England members. New England Anglicans, however, were largely Tory, and were so overshadowed by the Congregational tradition, and divided in their sentiments, as to be almost imperceptible as a group. The colonial victory left the Anglicans in disarray. Ironically, it was Connecticut-born loyalist Samuel Seabury who brought the church back to some semblance of order, becoming Bishop of Connecticut in 1784 and then the first Presiding Bishop of the new Protestant Episcopal Church.

The fifty years following the Revolution were ones of national stabilization and organization, and so it was with New England's religious groups. The Presbyterians were probably best situated as their very structure gave them the basis for a national organization, although the Methodists were the first actually to form a national body. The Baptists claimed a national identity and fought for the clear separation of church and state. The Quakers continued to look to England for their organized leadership.

The New England Congregationalists, now clearly the Yankee heirs to the Puritan tradition, stood dramatically apart from this emerging nationalism. With a kind of stoic self-assurance, now seen as typical of the Yankee style, the congregations energetically reasserted their independent ways. Their careful allegiance to old traditions meant the gradual decline of Congregational influence. As exploration pressed westward the Congregationalists entered into settlement agreements with the Presbyterians, in which the Congregationalists began to play a subordinate role. The tables had completely turned: in the colonial years, the Presbyterians had clung to the dominant New England church for protection.

A brief, and certainly not great, Second Awakening occurred at the end of the eighteenth century, spearheaded by Timothy Dwight, President of Yale and grandson of Jonathan Edwards. Eastern Massachusetts continued to be the center for more liberal Congregational thought. The removal of Trinitarian references from the liturgy at King's Chapel, Boston, in 1785, gave rise to American Unitarianism, later led by William Ellery Channing. Channing's unrelenting belief in man's worth through works led the way to the Transcendentalist movement. The early decades of the nineteenth century also saw the expanding influence of the Episcopal Church, which, in a return to its old Anglican form, garnered the membership of many civil and commercial leaders.

So Puritans became Yankees. The aggregation of small Puritan/Congregational communities would never again play the same critical role in American philosophical and intellectual development. The nationalization of an expanding country would help see to that. And yet that nation might never have bloomed without the tenacious, scrappy and independent thought these towns' meetinghouses produced. The Yankee triumphant was not a different species from his Puritan forebears, but rather a logical metamorphosis. He was certainly more openly materialistic, even sharp on occasion, and he completely rejected the Cambridge Platform's "Bible Commonwealth." He was, nevertheless, imbued with many a Puritan principle. Massachusetts and Virginia argue *ad nauseum* about which was the true cradle of the Revolution, each with reasonable cases, but there is no doubt that the irascible independence of the New England Puritan/Yankee was an essential ingredient. It is also certain that the New England Way, transformed and now spelled with a small "w", did not disappear.

14 Newport, New Hampshire: a 19th-century view of South Church (1725) and the parsonage.

III
GOD'S HOUSE
IN NEW ENGLAND

We love the venerable house
    Our fathers built to God
In heaven are kept their grateful vows,
    Their dust endears the sod.

They live with God, their homes are dust
    But here their children pray
And, in this fleeting lifetime, trust
    To find the narrow way.

R. W. Emerson
"The House our Fathers Built to God"
1st and last stanzas

Upon the hill they have a large square meetinghouse, with a flat roof, made of thick sawn planks, stayed with oak beams, upon the top of which they have six cannons, which shoot iron balls of four and five pounds, and command the surrounding country. The lower part they use for their church, where they preach on Sundays, and the usual holidays. They assemble by beat of drum.

Dutch trader's memory of Plymouth, 1677

Meeting was the glue which held together the early New England communities. Though the congregation's spiritual life was carefully prescribed from the pulpit, more secular aspects of community life led to a surprisingly democratic decision-making process. No issue was more hotly debated than the site for a new meetinghouse. The first meetinghouse of those early communities usually served as a fort or garrison as well, like the one in Plymouth described above. Its position was usually central and strategic. Even the placement of these defensively oriented structures sometimes aroused dispute, but the real debate usually erupted a few years later when, in more pacific times, a replacement was considered.

It was rarely considered calmly. Not only did all members have an opinion, but they all had to be heard. The examples of long-term wrangling are legion, and almost every town history includes at least one such dispute. If a parish was upgrading their meetinghouse, rather than replacing it out of immediate necessity, the debate could last for years. There were often as many as three or four suggested sites, each with passionate adherents. New England's largely agrarian economy meant that young towns spread out quickly, often covering many square miles of territory in a few years. It was not rare for families to travel miles on foot to go to meeting. This led to many a separatist movement when the topic of a new meetinghouse was raised. Rivers sometimes got in the way. While the first generation would settle on one side of running water, later families would often move across. The commute to meeting could be a damp and cold one. James Wellman of Windsor, Vermont, was renowned for appearing in his pulpit across the river in Cornish, New Hampshire, dripping wet. Final decisions on building often carried over from town meeting to town meeting, with motion after motion. There are examples of disputes being turned over to the Colonial civil authorities for resolution. Even then the decision was often ignored by the disgruntled members. General Court involvement, in fact, more often muddied the local waters than cleared them.

Decisions, however delayed, were eventually made, though sometimes for odd reasons. In Griswold, Connecticut, following General Court approval of the site favored by the minority, workmen began to dig a well. Apparent divine intervention led to the well wall's collapse and the immediate burial of all the workmen's tools. The alternative site was chosen. In Stratford, Connecticut, the minister, Israel Chauncey, gave up a year's pay to have his preferred location accepted. Richmond, Vermont, is another example of Yankee thrift in action. After years of debate the site was finally chosen because the land was given to the

15–17 An artist's impression of the three meetinghouses which preceded the present meetinghouse of the First Church, Hartford (1806). These resemble the three basic forms which were followed by the introduction of the church plan.

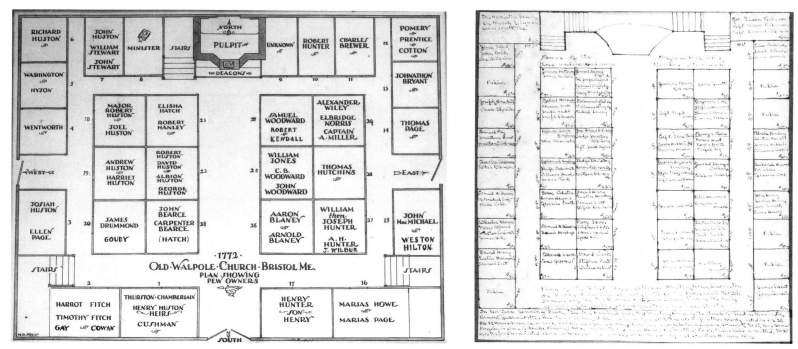

18, 19 Early pew plans of Old Walpole Meetinghouse, South Bristol, Maine (1772), and The Old First Church, Old Bennington, Vermont (1805).

town for that purpose. Tradition died hard: in some towns the new meetinghouse was built next to the old one, as in New Haven, Connecticut, and Rockingham, Vermont. Sometimes financial issues came into play, as in towns where dissatisfied citizens withdrew and formed their own parish but were still taxed in support of the old one. Decisions, once made in meeting, were not always final. Legend has it that in Rockingham, for instance, the minority moved all the building materials for the first meetinghouse to their preferred location the night before construction was to begin. A hastily-held meeting the next morning gave the energetic movers a victory. Unhappy losers often struck after the cornerposts had been set in place. The occasional fire was not unheard of.

Once the frame was raised, however, the discussion had only just begun. Where, pray tell, was everyone to sit? People could not be allowed just to wander in. The money raised for building the meetinghouse was gathered from the community, usually by selling or letting pews, which were guarded jealously and passed from generation to generation. Again, location was the primary issue. A Seating Committee was normally established which went about the earnest task of apportioning the benches or pews. As a general rule, in the early buildings the women sat on one side and the men on the other. The front pews were often reserved for the elderly. There was a special bench for widows, and the galleries were usually reserved for young men and women. Other status symbols, such as cushions, were sometimes provided for those who merited them. In most situations church members were responsible for their own footwarmers. Very few churches or meetinghouses had stoves before the early nineteenth century, and even then the installation was usually stoutly

20 The Old First Church, Old Bennington, Vermont: the gallery.

opposed by the elder members. The focal point, of course, was the pulpit, which rose above the congregation and had a sounding-board, an accoustic device above, and often a large window behind.

The distinction between a meetinghouse and a church needs some clarification. All the earliest Puritan houses of worship were meetinghouses, both because the buildings were used for all types of gatherings and because of a general aversion (as we saw earlier) to the word "church." The earliest Anglican churches were known as such, and were used for civil meetings only in the few communities where Anglicans were dominant—nowhere in early New England with the possible exception of Rhode Island. In later years the two terms became muddier in meaning and have often been used indiscriminately. In many present New England parishes, however, the careful distinction is still made between the church as an entity and the meetinghouse as a building, especially in parishes with an historic building to take pride in. From the mid-nineteenth century on, ecclesiastical buildings tended to be called churches, regardless of denomination, but during most of the years considered here, it was a distinction with a difference.

The earliest meetinghouses bore a resemblance to the fort-type meetinghouse at Plymouth. Most lacked cannon, and the roofs were not generally flat, but the stockade effect is appropriate. Many were surrounded by a palisade. A difficult balance between the pursuit of spiritual and temporal issues was maintained. These first structures, none of which survive, were usually temporary and quickly outgrown or outmoded.

Their replacements were mostly large, foursquare buildings with pyramidal or hipped roofs. They sometimes had gables, and were often topped by a belfry. The belfry served double duty as the spot where a bell or a drum summoned the townspeople, and as a lookout-post. Only one of these grand structures survives, The Old Ship Meetinghouse at Hingham, Massachusetts (1681). Most of these second-generation buildings had two stories, with a gallery around three sides at the second level. The seating was initially quite crude, just benches or logs propped on the floor, which were eventually replaced with box pews, designed for warmth in these unheated structures.

These foursquare buildings were constructed until the beginning of the eighteenth century, but were then gradually replaced by simpler, rectangular structures, with pitched roofs. These usually had three entries, with the pulpit on the long wall opposite the main entrance. Like their forebears, they usually had galleries, and eventually box pews. Though the variations were numerous, this oblong form became standard, Puritan in its "plain style" and, as always, with the pulpit as the centerpiece. Belltowers were first built nearby and later attached. The oblong form had many advantages, not the least of which was its simplicity. There are good examples of these buildings being expanded by splitting them in two and adding a central section, as was done in West Barnstable, Massachusetts.

You will read a great deal in this book about the meetinghouse and the church "plans." The transition from one to the other revolutionized ecclesiastical architecture in New England. Meetinghouses such as Hingham had the pulpit opposite the main entry. When the transition was made to the oblong meetinghouse, the pulpit and main entry remained

21 Trinity Church, Newport, Rhode Island (1725).

22,23 The fine pulpits at The Old Ship Meetinghouse, Hingham, Massachusetts (1681), and Alna Meetinghouse, Maine (1789).

opposite each other, but settled on the long side, or short axis, of the building. Even when steeples were built on, or added to, the end of Congregational meetinghouses, the main entrance remained on the long side (these towers often served as porch entries with stairway access to the galleries). Some of the earliest Anglican churches adhered to the meetinghouse plan. In the urban communities where the Anglicans took hold, however, they began to build churches more European in style and on the church plan, that is, with the main entry through the tower at the end of the building, and the pulpit and chancel opposite it on the long axis. As the eighteenth century progressed and more Congregational meeting-houses added towers or were built with them, the changeover to a church plan became inevitable.

The meetinghouse which Charles Bulfinch designed at Pittsfield, Massachusetts (discussed in more detail in the section on Lenox), and his building at Taunton, Massachu-setts, mark a major rural architectural shift in the late eighteenth century. The tower is incorporated in the building with a porch in front which serves as the main entrance to the meetinghouse. In these new buildings, which comprise the fourth basic stylistic group we will consider, a vestibule is housed in the entrance bay and under the tower, with an audience-room beyond oriented along the long axis of the building. The pulpit is opposite the entrance. Though the pulpit was sometimes built at the tower end, almost all these buildings were later switched to the more conventional form. The galleries remained, with stairway access from the vestibule. The sounding-board was often replaced by a large, domed ceiling. During the last decade of the eighteenth century, the church form became the standard.

In this book we consider these four basic types of meetinghouse. The first are the original stockade type, none of which are represented here, as none survive. The second are the large hip-roofed buildings, such as Hingham. The third are the oblong, pitched-roofed structures. The last group are the church-plan meetinghouses with incorporated towers, steeples, and almost endless variations. These last are the buildings which dominate the quintessential New England town green. The Anglicans, of course, built largely on the church plan from the start. Various of their buildings, such as those of Christ Church and King's Chapel, Boston, and Trinity, Newport, will be examined here.

Building a meetinghouse was no easy project, particularly in the rural communities. The taxes and pew costs represented a substantial commitment from these small settlements. Raising the building, though somewhat taxing too, was more pleasurable. It was much like any barn-raising, and was accompanied by the appropriate hoopla. Rum was almost always available to lubricate the process, though the combination of heavy timbers, great heights and alcohol was sometimes disastrous. All in all, it is remarkable how rarely these festive occasions ended with a tragic fall.

The first three types of meetinghouse were largely designed by itinerant or local joiners. It is important to note the skills of the master builders who led these projects, particularly in the case of the third group of buildings. Men such as Judah Woodruff of Farmington were talented joiners, builders and carvers who deftly drew their designs from combinations of buildings they knew, and introduced European motifs they had discovered in design-books. Woodruff's fine meetinghouse at Farmington, Connecticut, is included here.

In the cities, and largely in connection with non-Congregational buildings, we see the emergence of an American architectural school prior to the late eighteenth-century proliferation of the church plan. Peter Harrison of Newport and Joseph Brown of Providence are two prime Colonial examples. Though officially amateurs, their work is of the highest quality. Drawing on European designs, they produced American buildings, and their work set the stage for the emergence of the first great professional architects in the country following the Revolution. Harrison's King's Chapel, Boston, Touro Synagogue, Newport, and Brown's First Baptist Meetinghouse, Providence, are included here.

With the spread of the church plan, major design influences started to come from the new professional American architects. Bulfinch and his junior, Asher Benjamin, were probably New England's two most influential early professionals. Bulfinch's Boston work and his adherence to the church plan changed New England's ecclesiastical architecture for ever. Benjamin's *Country Builder's Assistant*—published at Greenfield, Massachusetts, in 1797— was the first American design-book, and it formalized and proliferated this architectural revolution. Once again drawing on European designs, these professionals took American architecture on a great forward leap, designing buildings ranging from Benjamin's baroque Old West Church in Boston to Bulfinch's First Church of Christ at Lancaster, which has some striking modernistic qualities.

24 The Old Ship Meetinghouse, Hingham, Massachusetts: view from the burial ground.

25 Old Meetinghouse, Rockingham, Vermont (1787).

26 Avon Congregational Church, Avon, Connecticut (1818).

27 Old South Meetinghouse, Boston, Massachusetts (1729): the steeple.

28 The restoration of the belltower in progress in the 1950s at West Parish Meetinghouse, West Barnstable, Massachusetts (1717).

29 First Church, Deerfield, Massachusetts (1824): a 19th-century view.

The master builder did not disappear. At First Church, Lancaster, the master builder, Thomas Hearsey, made important changes in Bulfinch's design: who then really was the architect, or was it more honestly a collaboration? Certainly, the Lancaster meetinghouse is known as the "Bulfinch Church." David Hoadley, a builder from Waterbury, Connecticut, is a classic case: he was, at the very least, an itinerant builder of some skill, but was he truly an architect? Did he become one in his later career? The meetinghouses of the United Church in New Haven and at Avon, Connecticut, where we know he played an important part, and the one at Cheshire, where he is purported to have done so, are all included here. Lavius Fillmore, who built the beautiful meetinghouse at Old Bennington, Vermont, is a further example. Though there seems to be little question that he drew his own designs, how did a rural builder become so proficient as early as his Connecticut meetinghouses indicate? Did he start as a builder, and teach himself architecture? Did Hoadley? (Abbott Lowell Cummings at Yale, and at least one of his cohorts, are working on the complicated issue of Hoadley now.) The evidence, as far as I could uncover it, is presented here, but with no intent to draw scholarly conclusions I am not qualified to make.

Let me conclude with a few notes. The interiors of these buildings have almost all been changed at some time, though many have been either wholly or partially restored. Wherever possible, I have tried to provide early photographs which illustrate the various stages, or at least to mention some of the changes. These changes, while rightfully disturbing to the preservationist, are sometimes quite intriguing and, even when almost unbearable, they are informative. They are certainly illustrative of changing taste. Painting is of particular interest, as many a pulpit wall was once graced with Victorian frescoes to decorate or imitate a chancel. This had less longterm detrimental effect than the pushing-out of the pulpit wall to build such a chancel, which was also fairly common. Many high pulpits were removed and replaced with low platforms. Box pews were almost universally replaced by slip pews during the nineteenth century. I have not chronicled the history of each parish's bells, though many a church history does. Suffice it to say that it is a very lucky, or inactive, congregation which has never had to recast its bell; also that Paul Revere was a far better silversmith than bellmaker. The buildings are given various dates at various times, sometimes based on when construction began, sometimes on the date of completion, and sometimes when they were dedicated or consecrated. I have elected to try to date all of them based on when construction began. As for the selection of buildings, I have tried to include a representative cross-section while allowing myself a degree of personal preference.

As with my previous book, which profiled a group of historic New England houses, I make no claim to break new ground. However, I hope that a look at the history of these communities and buildings, as well as some of the accessible information about their architecture, will illustrate something intriguing about New England's past. These are special buildings. Peter Benes points out that only one of an estimated 216 seventeenth-century buildings still stands, less than 0.5 per cent. Only 5 per cent of the eighteenth-century buildings survive. In any case, I hope that even those of you who have not seen the inside of a church lately will enjoy this trip "to meeting."

THE OLD SHIP MEETINGHOUSE

Hingham, Massachusetts 1681

In 1791, the citizens of Hingham determined that their meetinghouse had served its purpose. Alterations had been made both to the interior and the exterior on a number of occasions during its one hundred and ten years, but now they were resolved "to take down the old building and build a new one on its site." Town meetings had ceased being held there in 1780 and the church members probably felt that a building more in keeping with late eighteenth-century style was appropriate. Few of the first tall, foursquare meetinghouses were still standing when Hingham voted to demolish theirs. Happily, in 1792 they reversed their decision and voted to repair their meetinghouse instead, adding only one entry porch, with one false and two real doors. Whether they were motivated by an early preservationist impulse or the pressure of a lean year seems unimportant now. More than three hundred years after its construction Hingham's Old Ship stands as the only survivor of the second generation of meetinghouses which replaced the original fort-like houses.

The Hingham congregation had built a fort-like meetinghouse in 1635 on the arrival of Peter Hobart, their first pastor. His arrival may also have spurred them to change the settlement's name from Bear Cove to Hingham, after the English town from which Hobart and a number of the other settlers came. The original meetinghouse was surrounded by a palisade. This fort was used for secular and religious meetings, as well as for storage of powder and shot.

In 1678 John Norton, a graduate of Harvard, succeeded Hobart. Early New England ministries tended to be for the life of the minister and some divines served their parish for over fifty years. Hobart lasted forty-three, and Norton thirty-six years, while Norton's successor, Ebenezer Gay, tenaciously occupied the pulpit for over sixty years. We may, in fact, have Gay's long tenure to thank for the building's survival. One might surmise that the congregation would not have dared to demolish Gay's pulpit during the twilight of his ministry—which in his case lasted for thirty years. Not until four years after Gay's death was demolition even considered, and then it was rejected.

The present meetinghouse was built during the early years of John Norton's pastorate, raised between the 26th and 28th of July in 1681. It cost £430 and the funds were raised by taxing the citizens on the basis of their ability to pay. Apparently part of the palisade from the old garrison house was used in the construction of the new meetinghouse. There was some unhappiness, as usual, about the siting, because the majority chose not to build at the old site. The new meetinghouse measured 55 feet long by 45 feet wide, and had 31-foot eaves. The original roof was the typical tall-hipped variety, with three or four façade gables. The pulpit was originally on the north wall, though this was changed in a mid-nineteenth century remodeling.

The interior must have been striking in its simplicity. The original pews, as was often the case, were little more than benches. (Seating arrangements were, as always, a committee decision.) The oak framework of the building still takes one's breath away. The dramatic angles and curves of the high roof are particularly stunning. One explanation for the name of the meetinghouse is that the roof construction looks like an inverted ship's keel. The house may derive its affectionate nickname from its use as a sailors' landfall, as the similar meetinghouses in Scituate and Dorchester were traditionally known as the "Old Sloop" and the "Old Brig" for this reason.

The building was twice extended in the eighteenth century to accommodate population increases. The first alteration was in 1731 when the members also voted to close off the ceiling and thus disguise the remarkable framework. By 1734 the walls were plastered. The extensions involved pushing out the north and south walls, which changed the roofline. When

31 A 19th-century view of the interior, with slip pews and before the ceiling was removed.

32 The restored interior, with the ceiling removed and the box pews in place.

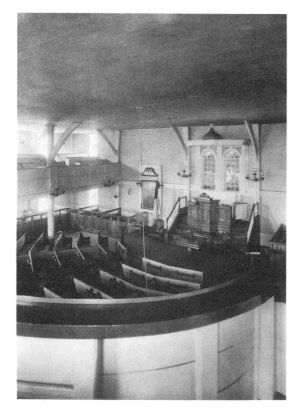

33 A side view: note the tall hip roof and belfry typical of the first square Puritan meetinghouses.

the second extension occurred in 1755 the pulpit was moved, the pulpit window installed and the east gallery was built. It was about this time that the first proper box pews were constructed and sold at public auction. General improvements and repairs were made at the time of near demolition, and in 1822 stoves were finally installed in Old Ship, then one of the largest and, presumably, one of the coldest meetinghouses in New England.

By 1869, the building was in need of major repairs. It had been built, not on a full foundation, but on stone laid on the ground. Consequently the floorboards and beams, the sills and supporting posts were rotting. One member of the congregation, General Stephenson, brought some flowers to the parish meeting which he explained he had plucked from the floor of his family's pew. A reconstruction which would eventually cost $7500 was approved by vote.

It was no small chore. The building was jacked up, the rotten members replaced, and it was then lowered on to an entirely new foundation. The box pews, the last of which had only been installed within the previous decade, were removed. They were replaced with curved Victorian pews, the ceiling was painted, the walls were papered in yellow print, the organ pipes became blue with gold decoration, the floor was carpeted and red drapes were hung. The interior of a Puritan ship became a Victorian palace.

In 1930 a restoration was completed which dispensed with most of the Victorian additions, returned some of the box pews and reconstructed the rest. Most importantly, the 1730 ceiling was removed, allowing the congregation to rediscover the wondrous framework of the roof. The restored church combines the best aspects of the seventeenth- and eighteenth-century parts of the meetinghouse.

The Old Ship provides a very special link to the Puritan past. Though it is important as an early Unitarian parish, it is also the one meetinghouse which survives from the seventeenth century. Hosea Sprague, a printer and printmaker in Hingham, wrote a nineteenth-century recollection of earlier days in town:

> I don't print for the Universalist or the Baptist; I print for the old fashioned religion such as I saw Dr Gay preach 57 years in the Old Meeting House, when he was 90 years old and wore a great white wig. Hingham was a quiet place 50 years ago, but for 20 years past my comfort has been very much injured by the ringing of the Baptist and Universalist bells every Sunday night and all other nights in the week. We have six meeting houses, five bells and 3500 inhabitants—700 to hear each bell.

Mr Sprague would probably find Hingham unbelievably noisy today, though in fact it is a quiet suburban town. But he would have no trouble finding his "Old Meeting House."

FRIENDS MEETINGHOUSE

Newport, Rhode Island 1699

Rhode Island has a liberal representation in this book because of its unique position in New England's religious history. Diversity and toleration were guaranteed in Rhode Island's 1647 code of laws which declared that "all men may walk as their consciences persuade them, every one in the name of his God." Here, thanks in large part to the arrival of Roger Williams after his banishment from Puritan Massachusetts, theology bloomed in colorful varieties which were hardly allowed to germinate during the early decades of the other colonies. The surviving religious buildings are a tribute to this theological diversity, represented in this book by the First Baptist Church in Providence (1775), direct descendant of Roger Williams's first Rhode Island church; St Paul's in Wickford (1707) and Trinity in Newport (1725), two of the American colonies' earliest Anglican churches; Touro Synagogue (1763), the United States' oldest surviving synagogue; and this old Quaker meetinghouse.

The Society of Friends, or Quakers, emerged from the left wing of English Puritanism. The movement's leader was George Fox (1624–91), a weaver's son who, early in his spiritual life, found even the dissenting churches unsatisfactory. Like Anne Hutchinson (another early outcast from Massachusetts) Fox determined that a person's relationship with the Almighty was individual and direct. He did not reject the Scriptures, but rather insisted that revelation must be an experienced reality. This experience often led to physical manifestations of emotion which inspired the term Quaker. Fox said that he "bid them

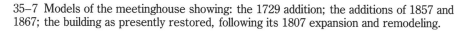

35–7 Models of the meetinghouse showing: the 1729 addition; the additions of 1857 and 1867; the building as presently restored, following its 1807 expansion and remodeling.

Tremble at the Word of the Lord." This understanding was not so distant from the Puritan ideal of "visible saints," and yet the Puritans, with their closely guarded congregationalism, found this individualistic religious manifestation threatening. The Society's teachings were viewed as undermining the ministerial, liturgical and congregational functions in the New England Way. The Quaker meeting was certainly different from its Puritan counterpart. The Quakers gathered in silence with the freedom for any member to speak if they chose, or the assembly might spend an hour in meditation. There was no provision for a sermon, the centerpiece of Puritan worship, and no minister to define the Way.

Quakers arrived in the Colonies from the middle of the seventeenth century, within a very short time of Fox's official founding of the sect. They were not always well received. When Ann Austin and Mary Fisher, two Quakers, arrived in Boston in 1656 they were jailed and later banished. When the *Woodhouse*, the Quaker *Mayflower*, arrived in New Amsterdam in 1657, its passengers received even harsher treatment than Austin and Fisher had in Massachusetts Bay. Six of their number reembarked and came up the coast where they were more warmly greeted. The Quakers found one segment of Rhode Island's population ready to embrace their philosophy. Newport and its environs became a center for New England Quakerism. A Monthly Meeting, which included Newport, Portsmouth, Jamestown and Tiverton, was established in 1658. The New England Yearly Meeting of the Society of Friends was held at Newport from 1661 until 1895—with a brief hiatus during the Revolution—and biennially until 1905.

There is little or no evidence of the first meetinghouse but it is assumed that one was built by the time George Fox himself traveled to Newport in 1672. This visit did much to spread the Quaker message, but it also brought out Roger Williams, then more than seventy, to do battle one more time. Though freedom of religious conscience was Williams's credo, he could voice energetic criticism when he chose. Fox had strayed, in Williams's view, too far

38 The simple barnlike façade of the Friends Meetinghouse.

into pantheism. The old spiritual warrior rowed alone thirty miles to Newport to do verbal battle. Fox had already left, but Williams debated with three earnest Quakers there and wrote his opinions in *George Fox Digg'd out of his Burrowes* (1676).

During the last quarter of the seventeenth century and the first half of the eighteenth, the Newport Quaker community flourished. Their position in society, commerce and politics was a leading one. By the end of the seventeenth century it was clear that a new building was necessary to house the Yearly Meeting. Though there are records of attendance reaching 5000, it appears that during most of the eighteenth century the yearly spring meetings were attended by about 2000 members. The meetinghouse, which came to be known as "The Great Meeting," was probably begun in 1699. Some of that original structure is included in the building as it stands today though there have been many additions and alterations. The old meetinghouse continued to be used for a few years after the Great Meeting was built.

In an excellent monograph, the architectural historian Antoinette Downing has traced the history of the 1699 meetinghouse from contemporary accounts. It appears that the first incarnation of the building was a large square meetinghouse with a hipped roof, probably much like the Puritan meetinghouses of the seventeenth century. There was a small addition built in 1705 which was apparently removed in 1729 when the first large addition, known as the North Meeting, was built because of increasing demand for space. The original section

40 The gallery steps in the 1729 addition. The removable panels behind open into the main meeting-room.

39 The Great Meeting in 1850.

41 The interior of the main meeting-room, with its plain benches.

was two stories high but open within while the addition had two stories, the second of which gave access to the main meeting hall.

The original section was described in 1702 as "large enough to hold five hundred persons or more, with fair and large galleries and forms or benches below." The second floor of the addition was probably used to seat the women during the Yearly Meeting and for regular local meetings. The first floor could be opened to the original Great Meeting by raising hinged dividers. This made the dimensions of the entire structure about 80 feet long by 50 feet wide. The shape of the meetinghouse following the 1729 addition was largely unchanged during the eighteenth century, though additional gallery space was added in 1743.

Newport's economic and social fabric was torn by the effects of the Revolution and the British occupation. The Quaker stand on pacifism left their leadership, particularly those holding political office, in a difficult position, though a doctrine of self-defense allowed for some participation in the struggle. After the Revolution, Quakers in Rhode Island never regained their previous status but the Yearly Meeting continued to be an important Newport event.

In 1807 a large section was added to the southern part of the meetinghouse to accommodate the Quaker annual gathering. The hipped roof was probably replaced at this time. How successful the enlargement was is dubious, judging from this account, in a letter by William Rotch after the Yearly Meeting in 1809:

> After Meeting I open my letter to add the addition to our Meeting House
> appears to make no difference & as many standing as formerly . . . 3000
> I conclude were in the house.

No other major changes were made until 1857 and 1867 when two more smaller sections were added. These have since been removed and the meetinghouse restored to the condition it was in between 1807 and 1857, and portions of all three of the earliest stages are visible.

Although it lacks the charm of the smaller rural Quaker meetinghouses, this is a building of importance. Though the number of Quakers in Rhode Island shrank dramatically during the nineteeth century (in 1905 the Yearly Meeting was moved to Providence), this barnlike meetinghouse played a central role in two hundred years of New England Quaker history.

ST PAUL'S CHURCH

Wickford, Rhode Island 1707

In 1701 Thomas Bray founded the Society for the Propagation of the Gospel in Foreign Parts (the SPG). It was an Anglican organization set up to foster the missionary work of the Church of England in the American colonies. Its aims were vastly different from the earlier Society for the Propagation of the Gospel in New England, set up in 1649, which, under the careful Puritan eye of John Eliot, had raised funds to assist his Indian missionary activities. Eliot wanted to spread the New England Way among the New England natives, while Bray wanted to invigorate the English Church in America.

Bray's success in New England was remarkable. As the fabric of New England's theology began to change in the eighteenth century, the Anglican Church made surprising

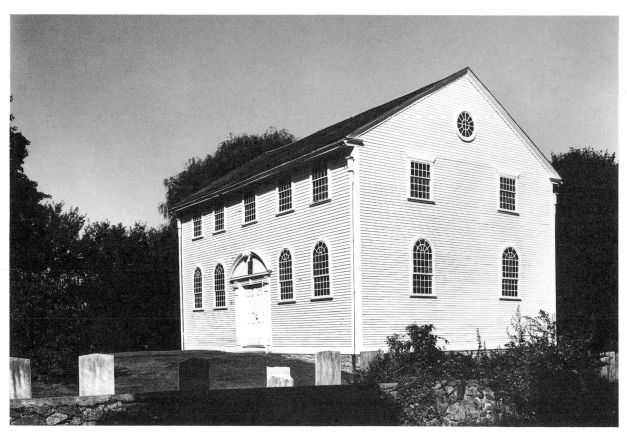

42 The façade at Wickford.

strides, particularly in areas where commerce was strong. Rhode Island, with its tradition of sectarian dissent, was early fertile territory, and it is here that we find the oldest Anglican church still standing in New England.

In 1702, a number of the Anglicans from Kingston, Rhode Island, on the western shore of Narragansett Bay, applied to the SPG for assistance in establishing their church. In 1707 they received a response in the person of the Rev. Christopher Bridge, sent by the Bishop of London to serve as Rector. In the same year, the congregation built St Paul's, five miles from where it now stands, near the main trail between New York and Boston.

The church they built was simple. It resembled its Congregational counterparts more than any surviving Anglican church in New England, and was quite probably a simplified version of the first church built by Trinity Parish in Newport. The graceful clapboarded exterior has roundheaded windows on the first story and a fine scroll-pedimented doorway, flanked by plain pilasters. The Rev. Bridge did not stay long, and the interior of this tiny church was not completed. The congregation then went without a minister, with the exception of one year, until 1721 when the Rev. James MacSparran arrived.

MacSparran was by all accounts a remarkable character. He was somewhat larger than life, weighing 300 pounds, and the reading desk at St Paul's had to be enlarged to accommodate him. Of Scotch-Irish descent, he had begun his career as a Congregational minister in Bristol, Rhode Island, but returned to England and was ordained in the Anglican priesthood. His size belied his energy. His diary makes it clear that he took his pastoral duties seriously, traveling many miles a week to visit and to preach. His parish originally extended from Narragansett Bay to the Connecticut border and from the Atlantic to the Pawtuxet Valley in the north. He preached in Warwick twice a month, and proudly claimed to

43 The dilapidated church, *c.*1860, before the steeple fell.

44 An early 19th-century pew plan, which indicates the ownership of pews *c.*1760. Note that the altar was at that time positioned at the east end.

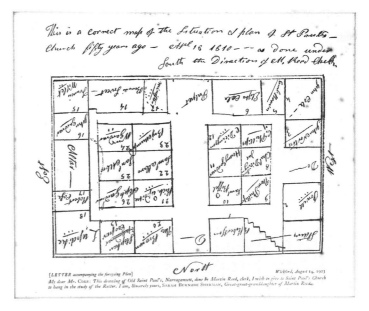

45 The double entry door with its fine scrolled pediment.

46 The altar and altar rail.

have been the first Anglican to preach at Providence. He liked to baptize converts by immersion in Pettaquamsett Pond and baptized slaves despite occasional opposition from some parishioners. MacSparran served St Paul's for thirty-six years and his drive and dedication are still legendary. On April 11th, 1756, during the last year of his ministry, MacSparran baptized the infant Gilbert Stewart (Stuart) at St Paul's. The painter's birthplace still stands, a short distance from the original site of the church.

During MacSparran's long tenure the interior was largely finished. The gallery was built in the early 1720s and there is a notation in the church records about the numbering of the pews which indicates that the first box pews were probably installed about this time.

MacSparran was minister during the heyday of the Narragansett country, when its plantations were most successful. It was also the most active period for St Paul's. During the Revolution the church was closed, with parishioners divided between the two sides, as in most Anglican parishes; it never regained its former vigor during the Colonial era. Kingston's population had also grown and shifted, and as early as 1765 there were disagreements concerning the location of the old church and the possibility of building a new one. The wrangling went on between North and South Kingston until December 1799, when the Northerners were allowed to move the old building up the road to Wickford, where it presently stands. There is an often-told tale which describes the North Kingstoners stealing the church on a cold January night and skidding it to Wickford. Apocryphal, no doubt, but indicative of the depth of the rift in the community.

The interior as presently restored is quite similar to a Congregational meetinghouse, with box pews below, benches above, a wineglass pulpit on the long wall opposite the main entry, and a reading desk in front of the pulpit. The gallery is supported by six simple columns and much of the framework of the pitched roof structure is visible. The altar table is on the west wall with the Wardens' Pews flanking it, though at an earlier date the altar was on the opposite side. The church records of 1804 indicate there were thirty pews which could each be let for one dollar per year. A steeple was added at the east end in about 1810. The stairway in the church, similar to the one in place today, was done away with and access to the gallery was built through the new steeple. Some other changes were made in the next forty years, but in 1847 a new church was built nearby and the old one fell into disrepair. In the middle of a clear calm night in late December 1866 the steeple fell, an event which for the rector of the new church across the street must have been a nightmare, but for the preservationist is a dream come true.

The Old Narragansett Church, as it is often known in deference to its young descendant, became delapidated during the latter half of the nineteenth and early twentieth centuries. Title passed to the Rhode Island Diocese in 1914, and the building was gradually restored. The church is open seasonally and some services are held there during the summer, but no visit is complete without stopping at St Paul's original site. "The Platform," as the spot is locally known, is where the parish's original cemetery is located, a tiny secluded burial ground with a memorial to the Rev. MacSparran and the tombstones of the founders of the church.

WEST PARISH MEETINGHOUSE

West Barnstable, Massachusetts 1717

47 The belltower.

In 1616 Henry Jacob gathered a dissenting congregation in Southwark, a village near (now part of) London. He described himself as "the rigidest sort of those that are called Puritans." In 1622 he left for Jamestown, Virginia, and was replaced by John Lothrop, a Cambridge graduate and Church of England minister who shared Jacob's "Congregationalist vision." Jacob and Lothrop both attempted the difficult course of alienating the established church while not entirely separating from it. The church at Southwark was at the forefront of Congregational polity, a tenuous political position which moved it inexorably toward conflict with the Church of England. In 1634, after much persecution and a stint preaching in prison, Lothrop and thirty of his followers sailed to Scituate, in the Plymouth Colony.

Lothrop kept a careful diary, much of which survives. His description of a December sabbath in their meetinghouse at Scituate could adequately describe hundreds of similar mornings in New England's frontier towns:

> December 22, 1636, in the meetinghouse, beginning some half an hour before nine, and continuing until after twelve o'clock, the day being very cold, beginning with a short prayer, then a psalm sang, then more large in prayer, after that another psalm, and then the word taught. Then making merry to the creatures, the poorer part being invited of the richer; after that prayer then a psalm.

48 Detail of the porch entry.

49 The restored interior.

50 The Revere bell. Paul Revere's records list the sale of a bell to West Barnstable in 1807.

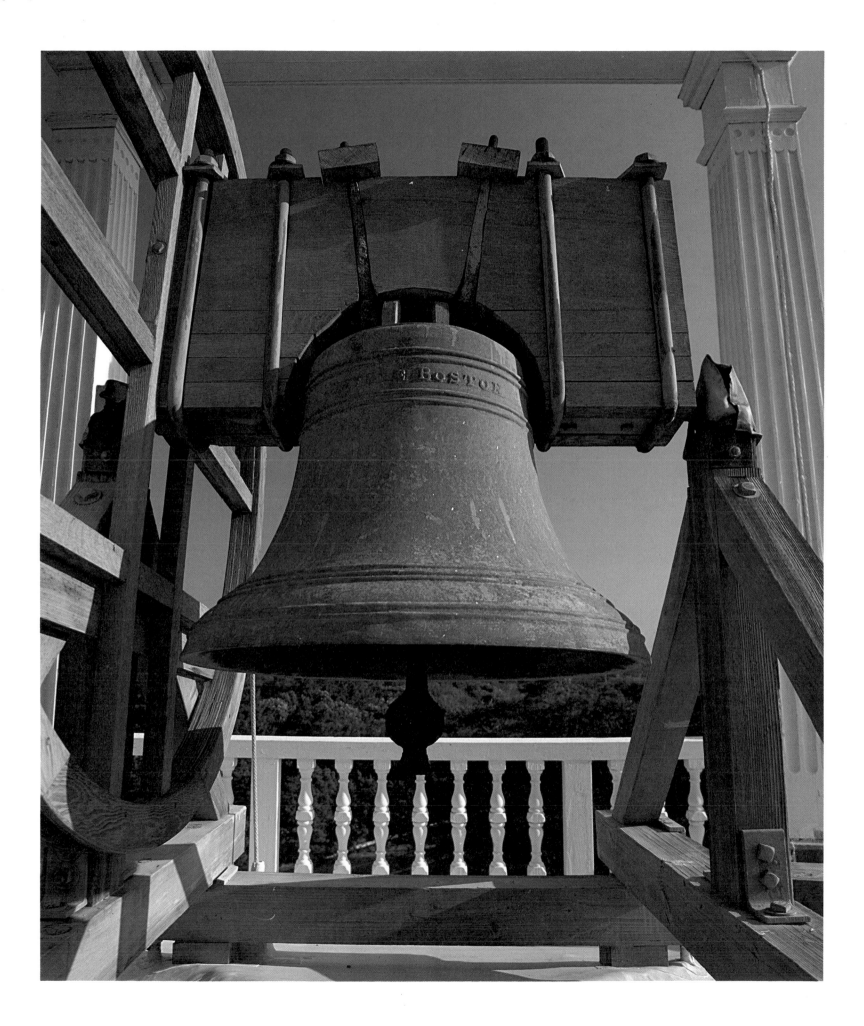

All was not "merry" in Scituate, however. There were rifts with other settlers, disputes about land and the inevitable doctrinal differences. When, in 1639, the Plymouth General Court offered Lothrop and his followers a suitable grant of land on Cape Cod, Lothrop urged them to accept. They had previously rejected another grant which he had suggested, but this one included good, cleared land and the congregation approved. Ola Winslow describes the journey of 1639, which was typical of many treks through the New England wilderness, though probably less arduous than some. "The road was a mere trail, sandy, swampy, hilly, through dense woods and along the shore; their destination a town of some dozen houses." They were clearly a contentious crew: the first meetinghouse was not built at Barnstable until 1646 partly because of the usual struggle about location. Until it was built the congregation put up with the cold and damp around Sacrament Rock.

The 1646 meetinghouse apparently served the parish until 1681, when a new building was raised. In 1708, during the ministry of Jonathan Russell, a group from Barnstable left to establish a church at Falmouth, but even this could not head off a new rift in the parish. By 1712, when Russell's son Jonathan assumed the ministerial duties at Barnstable, he did so knowing that the parish was likely to split, even though he adamantly opposed the schism. The town in fact split into East and West, and the West Parish Meetinghouse was begun in 1717, though the service was not held until Thanksgiving, 1719. Russell was forced to choose between the two, and when the West's meetinghouse was complete, he opted to be minister there even though he resided in the East, because there were in the latter:

> such a number who are so prejudiced or disaffected, and so set against me being
> there that my life is likely there to be rendered less comfortable to me, and
> perhaps my ministry less profitable to them . . . there is a very general if not
> universal desire in the West End that I should come to them.

The house the West Parishers had prepared for the younger Russell was a small, oblong one of the style which superseded the foursquare type, such as the Old Ship at Hingham. The main entrance was on one long side, with the pulpit wall directly opposite, and galleries above on three sides. It was, however, soon judged to be too small, and in 1723 the building was cut in half, and an extra eighteen feet was inserted. The belltower, one of New England's earliest, was also added either at this time or a few years later, and the weathercock which still stands on top of the tower was ordered from England. The only substantial change before the middle of the nineteenth century was a concession to contemporary style: the main entrance was moved from the side, in accordance with the traditional meetinghouse plan, and placed in the belltower, as usual in the church plan. This, however, was only a harbinger of things to come.

By 1852 Sandwich and the East Parish each had brand-new churches, and nearby Centreville had remodelled theirs. The West Parish—the church with the grandest tradition, having retained its claim to the Southwark lineage—was without a minister and its building was something of a poor relation. The parish was poor at the time, so it was decided to repair rather than replace the meetinghouse. It is unlikely that they had great feelings for the old

51 The meetinghouse as it appeared from 1852 until the 1950s. The 1852 instruction for remodeling stated that "all parts visible should be made new."

house as they determined that in their remodeling "all parts visible should be made new." The old belltower came down and was replaced by a nineteenth-century steeple and all the old framework was sheathed. The box pews disappeared and the walls were papered in a mottled pattern with borders of cherubs which were, to say the least, not of the Puritan taste.

Just over one hundred years later, after years of discussion and fund-raising, work began to restore the venerable meetinghouse to its former simple glory. The architectural detective work was painstaking. Examination of the original structure revealed the location of the old pulpit, sounding-board, the shape of the original gallery as well as the layout of the gallery steps right down to the height of the risers and the width of the tread. The reconstruction of the belltower was challenging but enough of the old tower had been used in the 1852 remodeling for the original shape to be determined, even to the placement of the windows. Nineteenth-century newspapers were combed in an attempt to trace pieces of the old construction sold at auction, no doubt to help fund the remodeling. Nearby houses offered up windows, pew spindles and panelling from the original meetinghouse, all of which were installed and reproduced. The ceiling, which was actually a 1723 addition, was removed.

Though we will see other examples of this simple oblong style, they are later and usually in comparatively remote settings, such as Rockingham, Vermont, and Alna, Maine. Hingham's Old Ship and the West Parish Meetinghouse are fine examples of the first two dominant styles in New England's true ecclesiastical architecture. West Parish also represents a remarkable piece of Congregational history which stretches back to the beginnings of American Puritanism and looks forward through the congregation still worshipping at West Barnstable today.

CHRIST CHURCH

Boston, Massachusetts 1723

If you hail a taxi in Boston and ask to be delivered to Christ Church you are likely to be greeted with a blank stare or, if you are not very observant, get dropped off in the wrong place. However, if you ask to be taken to Old North Church or even just wonder aloud where it was that the Lexington and Concord signal lanterns were hung, you will be deposited at the Christ Church door as swiftly as the traffic and the narrow streets of the North End will allow. Christ Church is an American icon of the first rank, a great patriotic symbol. Ironically,

53 The interior of Christ Church.

when it was built it represented a revolution of an entirely different order. In 1723 Christ Church was a symbol of proliferating Anglicanism in a city founded on Puritan principles. It was a monument to the church of the mother country in a colony which prided itself on its virtual commonwealth status.

To establish a parish which by its very definition was bound to create controversy, a rector capable of firm leadership was needed. In the Rev. Dr Timothy Cutler the founders of Christ Church, the first Anglican parish in Boston after King's Chapel, found a pastor who, while not pastoral in disposition, had some experience of being in the eye of a storm. He was born in Charlestown, Massachusetts, in 1684 and graduated from Harvard in 1701. He quickly established a reputation as one of the abler young preachers in the colonies. In 1710 he became Congregational pastor at Stratford, Connecticut, where he met his wife, the daughter of the Rev. Samuel Andrew, then Rector (President) of Yale College. His relationship with his predecessor probably helped insure Cutler's succession to his father-in-law's position in 1719. Ezra Stiles, who must have known Cutler in his later years and was himself President of Yale in the late eighteenth century, described Cutler in his *Literary Diary* as:

> an excellent linguist . . . good Logician, Geographer, and Rhetorician . . . in the Philosophy & Metaphysics & Ethics of his Day, or juvenile Education he was great . . . he was of an high, lofty & despotic mien. He made a grand Figure as the Head of a College.

It is clear that Cutler earned his position by merit as well as relationship, but he was destined to use his gifts to set Yale's Congregational polity on its ear.

The roots of Cutler's Anglican awakening are unclear. They probably stretch back to his parents who, while not Church of England members, were energetic loyalists. His connections in Connecticut were certainly a factor. The only Anglican parish (really a mission) in Connecticut when Cutler was there was in Stratford. The ministers of various Connecticut towns, including East Guilford, Killingly, Wallingford, Guilford and North Haven, all exhibited Anglican leanings. In 1722 Rector Cutler, together with Daniel Brown (they made up the entire Yale faculty), Samuel Johnson of Guilford and James Wetmore of North Haven, announced their intention of seeking ordination in the Church of England. After a hearing and public debate the trustees voted to "excuse the Rev. Mr Cutler from all further services as Rector of Yale College." Cutler went to England and returned in 1723 having received degrees from Oxford and Cambridge and ordination from the Bishop of Norwich.

When Cutler arrived back in Boston, he found an Anglican community that had survived its most trying time and was poised for a period of success that would last until the Revolution. The early history of Anglicanism in Boston is discussed in more detail in the section on King's Chapel. By 1723 the community was growing to the extent that a second parish, Christ Church, was needed, and yet another, Trinity Church, was destined to follow a little more than a decade later. Cutler's timing could not have been better. He served as minister at Christ Church from its founding until his death in 1765.

Just as the Anglicans of Boston looked to England for their leadership, the founders of Christ Church looked there for the design of their new building. There are many traditions concerning Christ Church's design. These include the long-held theory that William Price, a Boston publisher and print dealer, drew the plans, though twentieth-century scholarship has questioned the exact nature of his role. Anthony Blount was a Boston tallow chandler who together with Price was a member of Christ Church. Blount certainly took a great interest in the building and may have drawn the plans based on the Griffin-Hulsbergh print of Christopher Wren's St James, Piccadilly. He might well have acquired the print from Price. Price has been credited with the design for the original spire built in 1740. The influence of Wren is clear, and there have been many suggestions as to the specific derivation of the design. The choice of St James seems the most likely. The tower does bear some relationship to that of Wren's St Lawrence Jewry. But none of the relationships is as direct as Christ Church's certain parentage of Trinity, Newport. Christ Church is a Wren derivative expressed in a uniquely American, some might say provincial, fashion.

Regardless of who penned the elevations, the result is distinguished. The church's founders looked across the ocean for their design inspiration both as a statement about their theological orientation and as a signal to their Puritan neighbors. Nowhere in early New England is the differentiation between meetinghouse and church more distinct. The Boston building was built on the church plan, with the main entry through the tower and the wineglass pulpit and chancel at the far end of the long axis. The ceiling is barrel-vaulted with one long vault down the center and smaller vaulted arches over the galleries. The fluted columns, or piers, rise in two stages with the lower stage supporting the three-sided gallery. There are no shadow pilasters in the gallery, as at Trinity, Newport. High box pews were reinstated in 1912, when a major restoration was completed. The bricks for the exterior were fired in nearby Medford and the oak timber for the frame came from York, Maine.

Many aspects of the building were completed gradually during the twenty-two years following the laying of the cornerstone by the Rev. Miles of King's Chapel. The fine steeple, copied at Newport and Wethersfield, was not added until 1740. It has been toppled twice by hurricanes, and has twice been replaced. The first time, in 1804, it was restored by Charles Bulfinch. The church received the first peal of bells in Boston which were made in Gloucester, England, in 1745, and the present organ cabinet was made by Thomas Johnston of Boston in 1759. The chandeliers were first lit at Christmas 1724.

The preacher that night was sure to have been the Rev. Dr Cutler, and from the Christ Church pulpit he reigned as the dominant Anglican voice in Boston until his death. The parish faltered during and after the Revolution but managed, unlike King's Chapel, to retain its Anglican tradition, making the transition to the Protestant Episcopal Church in the 1780s. It is probably just as well that Cutler did not live to see the revolt; one can be reasonably certain he would not have been pleased.

TO THE GLORY OF GOD
AND IN LOVING MEMORY OF·
CORNELIUS VANDERBILT
BORN 1843   DIED 1899
WHEREFORE TAKE UNTO YOU
THE WHOLE ARMOUR OF GOD

TRINITY CHURCH

Newport, Rhode Island 1725

Christ Church, Boston, and Trinity, Newport, are evidence that New England's Anglicans brought modern European church architecture to the northeastern colonies. While the countryside was still dotted with simple barnlike meetinghouses, and long before this rural style changed substantially, these two urban churches set a new standard. Though the design of these early churches is known to have been influenced by the work of Christopher Wren, they have a distinctly American flavor. In the case of Trinity Church it is the vast expanse of clapboard that is intrinsically American.

St Paul's, Wickford, may have the oldest church, but Trinity, Newport, is Rhode Island's oldest Anglican parish. Newport's preeminent role in Rhode Island's economy makes this understandable, as Anglicans always seemed to thrive where business flourished. The parish was established in 1698, and its affairs were under the control of royal authorities in the person of Sir Francis Nicholson. The first church building was constructed in 1701 or 1702, soon after the founding of the Society for the Propagation of the Gospel in Foreign Parts: Trinity was the first parish to apply to the Society for aid. The Bishop of London sent a missionary rector almost immediately, but it was the arrival of the Rev. James Honyman in 1704 which solidified the parish. Honyman remained at Trinity until his death in 1750. There is no record of the first building, but it is suspected that St Paul's was actually modeled on Trinity's first church, and therefore that the Newport building was probably a somewhat grander version of the more provincial church at Wickford.

Despite Newport's present-day glamorous image, the pre-revolutionary eighteenth century was really Newport's golden age. As a colonial port, it ranked with New York and Boston. The town's economic growth coupled with Honyman's ministry led to the rapid expansion of the Anglican community. By the end of the first quarter of the century it was clear that the old meetinghouse would not serve. The present church is the result of this pressing need, although this church was also expanded later.

For an architect the congregation turned to Richard Munday, one of their own members. He is listed in various documents as a "house carpenter," and may also have run a tavern in Newport. He apparently built the Colony House and a number of private houses there. The architectural historian Norman Isham has suggested various Wren churches, the design of which may have influenced Munday. It seems certain, however, that the inspiration for Trinity, Newport, was Christ Church, Boston. The Newport church is basically a clapboard version of the Boston brick building, and the basic forms of the body of the church

55 James Honyman, Newport's
most important early rector: a
19th-century print.

56 A 19th-century view of the interior. Note the decorative painting highlighting
the ceiling arches.

and tower are strongly similar. Isham feels certain that Munday was sent by his employers to look at Christ Church.

The building was framed and covered by December 1725, and the interior was completed during the winter. The original structure was five bays long, with side entrances to the tower, unlike the front entrance at Christ Church. The round-headed windows are typical of the period.

The tower was a constant worry. The records show that Munday was called back and consulted on the problem in 1731, possibly after the tower had been struck by lightning. The spire which had been added to the original tower between 1745 and 1760 was, according to Isham, almost certainly a copy of the old one. In 1768 the tower was pulled down and replaced. The 1760s were years of change for the exterior of the church. In 1762 the two eastern bays were probably moved back and two more inserted, though Isham suggests that in fact the two were added on the end. The church had been originally limited by the extent of the church property, but the congregation's growth necessitated the later extension. The apse was probably added at this time.

Apart from the adjustments made to allow for the extra bays, the interior has been little changed. The column and gallery structure and panelling are very similar to Christ Church; the ceiling, however, is quite distinct. Though the overall form is similar, the center of the ceiling at Trinity is marked by the shallowest of groins, or what Isham calls a "very flat four-centered arch." The effect is handsome. The dominant feature of the church is the three-level wineglass pulpit, which is in the center aisle, unlike at Christ Church, where the pulpit

57 The wineglass pulpit at the head of the center aisle.

stands off to the side. The first level is for announcements by the clerk, the second for reading the lessons, and the bowl of the wineglass is for the sermon. The sounding-board hangs above the uppermost level.

The original oak altar-table stands in the chancel at Trinity. Discarded in 1837, it was returned in 1920. George Washington worshipped at Trinity during three visits to Newport, and his pew by the lower level of the pulpit is still reserved for visitors. Newport's later nineteenth-century summer seasons are also clearly represented in this old church, most visibly in the stained-glass windows installed in the lower level. These memorials are remarkable; the examples of Tiffany workmanship in particular are superb. One of the memorials is to Godfrey Malbone, an important merchant and vestryman during the middle of the eighteenth century. Malbone was famous for his sharp business practices and excellent parties. Like most good New England Anglicans, he was an ardent Tory. During dinner one evening Malbone was informed that an angry rebel mob had set fire to his house. In typical fashion he asked all his guests to join him on the lawn, where they finished dinner while the house burned to the ground.

The organ case at Trinity is of interest as it is the original case for the organ donated as a token of friendship in 1733 by the Anglican philosopher Dr George Berkeley. Berkeley spent time in Newport after being driven ashore on his way to Bermuda; he befriended the Rev. Honyman and remained in Rhode Island for three years. Berkeley had first apparently offered the organ, for obvious reasons, to the congregation at Berkeley, Massachusetts. They rejected his offer with typical levity, calling the organ "an instrument of the devil for trapping men's souls."

58 Detail of a doorway showing the rare pediment form employed in the entrances to the church.

OLD SOUTH MEETINGHOUSE

Boston, Massachusetts 1729

In the late 1660s the First Church of Boston determined to call as pastor Jonathan Davenport of New Haven. The majority vote enraged the minority in the parish. The issue was doctrinal, with the recently introduced Half-Way Covenant at the root of the problem. Davenport was one of the first generation of orthodox New England divines and he was energetically opposed to the Covenant's compromise. The vocal minority disagreed—not only on doctrinal grounds but also because of Davenport's advanced age—and their secession led to the organization of the Third Church of Boston (the Second Church having been founded in 1650). This Third Church, which came to be known as Old South, was born out of controversy and in its first hundred and twenty years delighted in standing on the knife-edge of conflict.

An early view of Boston, by Boston printer and bookseller William Price, gives us the best picture of what the first South meetinghouse, built in 1669, was like. It was a large gabled building with a turret above. A seventeenth-century description calls it "a large spacious and faire meeting house with three large Porches," and the same account notes the cost at "neare if not above 2000 pounds." An early nineteenth-century history says that it was built of cedar "with a steeple, galleries, square pews, and the pulpit in the side as in the present buildings." The early years in the first meetinghouse were important ones. Samuel Willard, a prolific writer who energetically opposed the excesses of the Salem witch-trials, and Thomas Prince, the famous New England historian, were both early pastors of Old South and Judge Samuel Sewall, the diarist, was a prominent parishioner.

By the 1720s the parish was well enough established to consider a new and larger meetinghouse. Some excerpts from the carefully preserved church records give a clear indication of when the crucial decisions were made. February 27, 1728: "This question was put to the Brethren; Whether it was their mind that this House should be repaired and enlarged; or a new Meeting House Built ... There were twenty ... for repairing and enlarging ... forty-one for building a New Meeting House." April 23, 1728: "That the New Meeting House be set upon that place on which the old House now standeth." June 26, 1728: "That the New Meeting House be built with Brick." February 18, 1729: "That the committee for Building ... be impowered and directed to take down our present Meeting House, as soon as conveniently may be after the 24th of this Instant, February." The following vivid description of the demolition of the old meetinghouse appeared in the *Boston News-Letter* of March 6th:

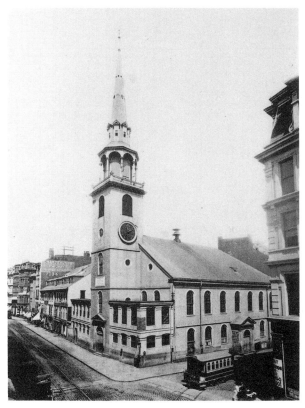

59 Old South in its present Boston surroundings.

60 Old South in the latter part of the 19th century. Note the additions, inserted at the sides of the tower, which have since been removed.

On the Monday, the Workmen took down the Windows, the Pews, the Pulpit and the Seats bothe below and in the Galleries. On the Tuesday in the Fore noon, they took down the Belfry, the Porches, the Stairs and the Galleries themselves. In the Afternoon they drew off the Boards at bothe ends and laid it open; and about Five o Clock, they turned over the whole remaining part of the Building at one Draught into the Yard on the North Side; in doing which it fell all to pieces. Yesterday they employ'd in removing the Fragments. And when we came to examin the main timbers, it was surprizing to see the Bottom of Great Rafters which upheld the Roof, together with the hinder Beams which bore up the Galleries were quite decay'd with Rotteness; and the Ends of all the Summers, for Six or Eight foot were in a great measure turn'd to Powder; that nothing but the King-posts and the other Frame above has for a long time kept them from tumbling down upon the People. And it seems to be a wonderful Providence that the last Lord's day especially, when it was so much crowded, that the whole Congregation was not buried in a heap of Ruins.

The brick meetinghouse which rose in its place is one of the largest meetinghouses ever built in New England, oblong in form, 94 feet long and 67 feet wide. It is also tall enough to house two levels of galleries. In its exterior it is a larger cousin to Christ Church, or Old North, built in the North End of Boston six years earlier. Both are of red brick, have ranks of round-headed windows and a similar basic form, but there the similarities cease. Despite its steeple, Old South is in every way a meetinghouse while Christ Church is definitely a church. The main entry at Old South is on the side with the pulpit opposite and two ranks of galleries above. Benjamin Winsor described the original interior in 1830:

It was finished with two galleries as at present; and the pulpit in the same position as now, but larger and higher than this, with a sounding board projecting from the wall above the casing of the window; and with two seats directly in

61 One of the plans to save the meetinghouse, dated February 1878, after the congregation had departed.

62 Detail of the pulpit.

front, one somewhat elevated for the deacons, and one still more elevated for the elders. On each side of the middle aisle, and nearest the pulpit, were a number of long seats for aged people; and the rest of the floor, except the aisles and several narrow passages, was covered with square pews.

The steeple, Old South's most distinctive feature, has an octagonal open-arched belfry stage with an eight-sided spire rising above. Each segment of the spire's roof has a gable. It is not as radical a departure as might first appear if considered in context. It is really a wider, elongated version of the turret belfries and spires which appeared in many late seventeenth- and early eighteenth-century meetinghouses. The steeple at Hingham is an example. In 1712 the last of the great Boston meetinghouses of the older style, the long-gone "Old Brick," had a belfry and spire very similar to the steeple at Old South.

It was during the turbulent years prior to the Revolution that Old South returned in spirit to its contentious roots. No colonial meetinghouse played so great a political role. From 1770 to 1775 the Old South hosted many critical meetings of the period. It was here that John Hancock, Joseph Warren and others annually recalled the Boston Massacre, and it was here that the meeting which preceded and inspired the Boston Tea Party took place. Warren's final oration on the fifth anniversary of the Massacre was attended by an overflow crowd. He said:

> Our wish is that the British and the colonies, may . . . grow in strength together. But if these pacific measures are ineffectual, and it appears that the only way to safety is through fields of blood, I know you will not turn your faces from your foes.

The thirty or forty British officers present moaned audibly as Warren finished. Within weeks Warren's wish was dashed. The British leadership took peculiar revenge on the building: they tore out the downstairs furnishings and turned the meetinghouse into a riding school. One of the Deacon's pews became a pigsty. Apparently, when the siege of Boston was over, Washington, an Anglican, stood in the gallery reviewing the destruction and said: "Strange that the British, who so venerated their own churches, should have desecrated ours."

British army riding practice was not the last indignity the venerable building suffered. One hundred years after Warren's oration the parish moved and for some time the meetinghouse was threatened with demolition. In 1877, twenty Boston women purchased the building. They managed to prevent its destruction, and the Old South Association was formed. The meetinghouse has since served as a museum, a post office and is now, in largely restored form, again a museum.

KING'S CHAPEL

Boston, Massachusetts 1749

The Puritan attitude to other Protestant dissenters has been discussed in some detail. However, their attitude toward their Anglican brethren was, if anything, even more complex. The story of this difficult interrelationship looms large in the history of King's Chapel, the first Anglican parish formed north of the Mason-Dixon line. In Massachusetts Bay the Puritan ideal had been given independent life, and yet the relationship with the English overlords was always something of a tug-of-war, even during Oliver Cromwell's Puritan ascendancy. Moreover, the Puritans had no more formally separated from the established church than they had from England, and yet they were separate both in reality and in attitude. How then were these Puritan independents supposed to greet the ordained representatives of the established church from the mother country?

When the Rev. Robert Ratcliffe arrived in Boston in the late spring of 1686, his reception was very mixed. Much of the colonial and military establishment, as well as many of the leading members of the commercial community, were Anglicans. In many communities the merchant leaders leaned toward the established church, both because of Puritan uncertainty about the questions of morality and profit and because of familial and business ties with England. These leaders in Boston greeted Ratcliffe with open arms, but their more numerous Puritan counterparts were less sanguine about Ratcliffe's proposed ministry. They could not banish him—though one can be sure many were inclined to—but they certainly did not make life easy for him. Nevertheless, on June 6th Ratcliffe held his first service in the Town House, and on June 15th King's Chapel was established.

63 The steepleless façade of King's Chapel, photographed *c.*1900.

65 The pulpit and sounding-board.

66 Detail of the carved capitals in the gallery.

The search for a perfect place to house the church was frustrating; tensions were exacerbated by the Puritans' conviction that the colonial ministers favored the Anglicans. It was suggested that the Puritans give up a meetinghouse to the Anglicans, and even that the dissenting community should help support the new church. Soon after his arrival in late 1686, Governor Edmund Andros, the overseer most despised by the Puritans, had decided that the Anglicans should be allowed to share South Meetinghouse, and within the year he appropriated a corner of the cemetery nearby, so that Ratcliffe's congregation could build there. Even Andros' expulsion following the Glorious Revolution in England of 1688—when the Catholic James II was deposed—could not stop the completion of the first King's Chapel, and the present building stands partly on the land he appropriated.

The last years of the seventeenth century were difficult and critical ones for King's Chapel, but the new century was kinder to the parish. The Congregationalists were in

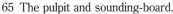

64 The gallery: note the shadow pilasters and groined arches.

turmoil, the best and luckiest of Boston's merchants prospered and the Anglican Church, while still small in relative numbers, thrived. The Great Awakening swirled through New England, but left little impression on King's Chapel. George Whitefield and Charles Wesley worshipped there, but they never entered the pulpit. In 1747 the English-born Yale graduate Henry Caner took over a healthy and growing parish, which Caner and most of his congregation surely viewed as an island of social and religious sanity in a choppy Puritan sea.

One of Caner's first projects was to build a new church which would both accommodate the church's increased population and solidify its social standing. Peter Harrison of Newport was chosen as architect. Like all the gentleman architects of his day, he made his money in other pursuits and was therefore prepared to donate his services. His credentials to date were slim, but then Caner was not asking too much of him. The rector wrote to the architect in April 1749 that "we do not require any great Expense or Ornament, but chiefly aim at Symmetry and Proportion." In September of the same year Harrison sent the plans with these comments in his covering letter:

> Since I first undertook to draw a Design for the New Church, many things have
> unexpectedly occurred to prevent me from finishing in the time you requested
> . . . I now send you by the Post Rider all the Plans & Elevations . . . which I
> should be glad to hear answers your expectations, & that no material alteration
> is made in the Execution, as it is very possible by that means the Symmetry of
> the whole may be destroyed.

Harrison's plans were certainly worth waiting for. Their grand symmetry must have far exceeded the hopes of the Rev. Caner. The resulting building certainly marks a turning point in New England church architecture; and its construction established Harrison as the region's premier colonial architect, a position he confirmed with the designs for buildings such as Christ Church, Cambridge (1760), and Touro Synagogue (1763).

The exterior, of Quincy granite, is simple and has actually never been finished. Due to lack of funds, the steeple was not completed. The colonnade was built later and of wood, though it follows Harrison's specifications. It is intriguing that Christ Church in Cambridge mimics this steeple-less style. For the interior, Harrison drew heavily on designs from across the Atlantic, to create a space which seems simultaneously to meet Caner's request for simplicity and also triumphs in its elegant details. The simple but fine panelled pews contrast with the pairs of fluted Corinthian columns which rise above them. The tall gallery windows light the nave from above, and the simple chancel stands behind the fine wineglass pulpit. The elegant dignity of the Governor's Pew leaves no doubt as to who it was designed for. The harmonious amalgam which Harrison achieved here is the hallmark of his work.

Harrison's new church was actually built around its smaller predecessor. When the basic construction was completed the old church was dismantled and the pieces pitched out of the windows of the new building. The church was officially opened, even though it was not yet finished, in August 1754. Though the hot issue of episcopacy precluded the ordination of an

67 The chancel and pulpit.

68 A 19th-century view from across the burial ground.

American Anglican bishop before the Revolution, there can be little doubt that had there been such an office-holder King's Chapel would have been his cathedral.

The Revolution was disastrous for the Anglicans of King's Chapel as elsewhere in New England; many were Tories, and most were divided in their loyalties. In 1776 some parishioners joined the Tory exodus which followed the Patriot siege, though most of the congregation elected to stay. Henry Caner was among those who left, and the ones who stayed endured a rudderless Revolution.

At the end of the War the New England Anglican community was in disarray, and the congregation of King's Chapel had to search for a theological identity. In 1782 they called an interim minister named James Freeman, a Harvard graduate who had survived the Revolution as a nominal patriot. He had not enlisted in the Continental Army, but had spent two years in a British prison largely because of his father's residence in Quebec. After six months the congregation asked him to stay, despite his warning that his religious ideas might be difficult for them to swallow. Freeman embraced a liturgy which was an outgrowth of liberal Congregationalism, Anglican in form but which rejected the deity of Christ and thus the Trinity. The parish accepted the liturgy he designed, and as a result the American Unitarian Church, drawing on old European roots, was born. When the Protestant Episcopal Church emerged in the 1780s as the descendant of English Anglicanism, Freeman's attempt at a rapprochement was rebuffed. The differences were too great. The King's Chapel liturgy represented a unique New England alchemy, well and simply described in André Mayer's excellent monograph on the church as "Unitarian in theology, Anglican in liturgy and congregational in church government." Rarely has one building been so prominently linked with two theological eras as Harrison's colonial masterpiece.

TOURO SYNAGOGUE

Newport, Rhode Island 1763

The doctrine of toleration upheld in Rhode Island attracted all manner of people searching for freedom of religious expression. The Jews who came to Newport were Sephardim, who had enjoyed great freedom during five hundred years of Moorish rule in Spanish territories. The success of Ferdinand and Isabella in recapturing Spanish territory and the horror of the Inquisition that followed caused many of the Sephardim to seek refuge in Holland, England and the Dutch colonies. Some came to the American colonies, where they gathered congregations in New York and Newport. Their Spanish roots are referred to in Longfellow's "The Jewish Cemetery at Newport":

> The very names remembered here are strange,
>   Of foreign accent, and of different climes:
> Alvares and Rivera interchanged
>   with Abraham and Jacob of old times.

69 The façade of the synagogue, with the ell beyond.

The congregation in New York predates Newport's, but New York's first synagogue is long gone. Touro stands as the only colonial synagogue in the United States.

The Jews were among the earliest settlers of Newport, with records of their residence stretching back as far as 1658. In 1679 there is a record of the Jews and the Friends together buying land for the cemetery which later became the subject of Longfellow's poem. Between 1680 and the Revolution the Jewish community grew and prospered, attracting new immigrants by their own success in Newport's marketplace and by asking for and receiving the continued protection of the colonial government. They helped pioneer the manufacture of soap, spermaceti candles, potash, snuff and built iron and brass foundries. They also produced some of Rhode Island's most outspoken Revolutionary patriots.

For the first hundred years of their residence in Newport the Jews worshipped in private homes. In 1759 they purchased a lot on what is now Touro Street with the intention of building a synagogue. Peter Harrison, gentleman architect of Newport, was asked to design the building and as usual he donated his services. Harrison designed a number of buildings in Newport, including the Redwood Library (1748), the Brick Market (1761) and various residences. The simple colonial style of the Touro Synagogue was one of his finest efforts.

The synagogue is square, with an ell, and is set at a sharp angle to the street. The angle allows the Holy Ark to face east, toward Jerusalem. The structure is of brick, though it is painted yellow ochre with brown trim. In basic from it bears a similarity to the Anglican church which Godfrey Malbone, Jr built at Brooklyn, Connecticut, seven years later, and Malbone had undoubtedly seen Harrison's work. The interior certainly shows the influence of various design-books, particularly in the crafting of the Ark, which is a fine Georgian cupboard. The gallery is unusually detailed, with twelve sets of columns (Corinthian over Ionic) which represent the twelve tribes of Israel. There is also a certain Spanish colonial feel to the overall shape of the building and some similarity to the synagogue built in Amsterdam by the Sephardic refugees in 1675. One comes away with the overwhelming feeling that Harrison has managed to incorporate a wide variety of cultural, historical and architectural influences with consummate skill and a wonderfully harmonious result.

The cornerstone was laid in 1759 by Aaron Lopez and Jacob Rodriguez Rivera, and the dedicatory Chanukah service was held on December 2nd, 1763. The service was performed by Rabbi Isaac de Abraham Touro, after whom the synagogue was named. The building was more than a house of worship to this community. Like many meetinghouses, it was an important symbol. To Newport's Jewish community it represented an end to transience and was a recognition of the community's stability and role in Newport's successful pre-revolutionary life.

This vision was to be shortlived, shattered this time not by persecution, but by Newport's post-revolutionary collapse. The congregation dispersed, Rabbi Touro moved to Jamaica, and by 1782 virtually all remnants of the old congregation had disappeared. There was no way of meeting the required quorum of ten in order to hold services and the synagogue was closed. It was, however, used for early sessions of the Rhode Island General

70 The interior looking towards the Ark. Note the fine carving throughout.

Assembly (1781–4) and Supreme Court sessions. In 1790 President Washington visited the synagogue and met with the remnants of the congregation.

Exhibiting a remarkable sense of self-preservation, which their Yankee brothers might more often have emulated, the scattered segments of this community determined to maintain their synagogue. They were led in this by the generosity of Rabbi Touro's sons Abraham and Judah, who gave funds to preserve the old building even during the years it remained closed. Judah Touro's generosity extended toward many efforts and all religions— but when he died his remains were brought to Newport from his home in New Orleans for burial in the Jewish Cemetery. The 1854 funeral was a major Newport event. Happily, when in the 1880s the community was once again large enough to support an active synagogue, this fine building was waiting. During the 1960s some restoration took place, though little was necessary. Some pews which had been added in 1900 were removed, and the interior woodwork was repainted. The exterior paint was retained partly because sandblasting might have damaged the original brick. The synagogue has come to represent to the present American Jewish community what it originally meant to its Newport builders: it is a symbol of permanence and freedom.

When Washington visited in 1790 he was addressed by Moses Seixas, a community leader. Washington borrowed from Seixas in his response when he stated that the United States Government "gives to bigotry no sanction, to persecution no assistance" and requires, in his own words, only that people "demean themselves as good citizens." Washington concluded:

> May the Children of the Stock of Abraham, who dwell in this land, continue to merit and enjoy the good will of the other Inhabitants; while every one shall sit in safety under his own vine and figtree, and there shall be none to make him afraid. May the father of all mercies scatter light and not darkness in our paths, and make us all in our several vocations useful here, and in his own due time and way everlastingly happy.

71 Detail of a Corinthian capital in the gallery.

OLD TRINITY CHURCH

Brooklyn, Connecticut 1770

The Anglican church at Brooklyn, Connecticut, is a classic example of how dissention and divisiveness built many New England churches and meetinghouses. Godfrey Malbone, arch-Tory, Anglican and vestryman, was prominent both in the history of that parish and the town. Educated at Oxford, he sent his son Godfrey Jr back to England for his education. When Godfrey returned he found that his father had suffered some serious financial reverses, as was often the case with those of the Newport traders who trod a fairly fine line between merchant and privateer. In the circumstances the father decided it would be wise to send his son to manage his 1200 acres of farmland in Brooklyn (then Pomfret), Connecticut, which he had bought in 1740 from Connecticut Governor Belcher, and which had originally been part of an English Puritan grant. Godfrey Jr arrived in Brooklyn in 1766 with his wife and twenty-one slaves in tow. In education, style, religion and world view the son was much like the father.

About twenty-five years earlier another, very different gentleman had come to occupy the other acres of this same large Brooklyn grant. His name was Israel Putnam. Putnam was a man of tremendous personal courage and limited education, who later achieved great fame in the French and Indian and Revolutionary Wars. During his years at Brooklyn he had prospered as a farmer and tavern keeper. The two must have regarded each other warily. Putnam was a New England Congregationalist from Danvers, Massachusetts, soon to be a Patriot; Malbone, with his Virginia-born father and southern wife, could not have been more firmly rooted in the Colonies' staunchest Church of England tradition. They were destined to clash and what could have made a more appropriate focal point than the decision to build a new Congregational meetinghouse?

The meetings to discuss repair or replacement of the then thirty-two-year-old meetinghouse may well have been spurred on by the arrival in town of its biggest taxpayer. Legally Malbone was liable for taxation in support of the project, despite his standing as an Anglican. In 1766, Putnam's Congregationalists voted to rebuild, but at another meeting in 1768 attended by a persuasive Malbone, they were convinced that repairing the old building would be sufficient. Putnam, representing the town in the Connecticut General Assembly, led the opposition to Malbone in arguing for a new meetinghouse. In 1769, a meeting was held at which the previous year's decision was to be reviewed. Malbone's arrival at the meeting proved that he had inherited more than an education and religion from his flamboyant father: he was conveyed to the gathering on a sledge pulled by twelve streamer-bedecked oxen, and was then carried into the meeting, apparently in a sedan chair, by his slaves. Despite this grand performance the vote turned against him. Malbone's levy for the new building was set at approximately one-eighth of the total cost. One can only imagine the Newport gentleman's fury at having to pay £200 to build a country church he could hardly bear to worship in. Malbone, however, had not played his last card.

According to Connecticut law all were liable for taxation to support the town meetinghouse unless they could demonstrate allegiance to another organized parish. Since there was no Anglican church in the vicinity, Malbone determined to create one. In November 1769 Malbone gathered his few fellow Anglicans and founded Trinity Church in honor of his home parish in Newport. Though his appeal to the Society for the Propagation of the Gospel was passed over, probably due to rising unrest in the colonies, Malbone was not deterred. He was determined to build the church and although he raised some funds from Newport, Boston and New York friends, he must have ended up spending a good deal more than £200 in the construction and support of it. Malbone himself drew the plan and oversaw the construction which began in June 1770.

72 Brooklyn's Unitarian (originally Congregational) meetinghouse, on the green—the building which Godfrey Malbone refused to pay taxes to support.

73 An early 20th-century postcard showing the shutters which have since been removed.

74 Trinity Church from the burial ground.

His design drew heavily on his Newport upbringing, and though he was no architect he chose fine masters to emulate. The basic form for both the interior and the exterior was modeled on Harrison's Touro Synagogue. The exterior is proportioned almost as Touro, without the ell. The arrangement of the round-topped windows is slightly different, and Malbone's lower rank of windows is foreshortened. The pedimented doorway resembles the pedimented entry at Touro. The interior of Trinity has a fine simple provincial style which is as much a tribute to Harrison's artistry at Touro as to Malbone's tenacity in Brooklyn. However, Harrison's mastery of detail is lacking: it is hard to look at Trinity's interior without superimposing Touro's Corinthian columns, carved railings or dentiled cornices. The two buildings are at once so similar in form and so different in effect.

Malbone's plan reveals his most important Newport influence (other than perhaps that of his father). Completely unlike Touro, the layout resembles the front pews at Trinity, Newport. At Brooklyn the box pews move back gracefully, becoming wider while the lone center aisle shrinks. Originally the church had a wineglass pulpit like the one at Newport; one can still see the mark in the floor where it stood. Though some changes have been made to the chancel, Malbone's church is largely as he built it. It is set outside the town and is surrounded by a lovely churchyard.

Godfrey Malbone received his tax bill in late 1770, but he never paid it. His church was actually completed a few months before its Congregational counterpart. The meetinghouse, set literally in the center of Brooklyn, is also a notable building. It is a side-entry meetinghouse with the pulpit opposite the door. The lower rank of side windows and all the end and tower ones are pedimented to match the doorway. In most respects the exterior is similar to the First Church in Farmington (1771), though the proportions of the Brooklyn steeple are not quite so fine. The original steeple was lost in the 1938 hurricane, and the replacement is not an exact copy. The interior has been recently restored.

There is a postscript to this tale: Daniel Putnam, Israel's son, married Malbone's daughter and he later became senior warden of Trinity. This accounts for the plethora of Putnams and Malbones lying nearby in the cemetery. A new stone church was built in 1865 near the town green. The parish still maintains the cemetery and old building which is locally and fittingly known as the "Malbone Church."

76 A 19th-century watercolour of the "new" brick Trinity Church.

75 The interior looking towards the entry door. The cut in the flooring where the wineglass pulpit once stood is visible in the foreground.

FIRST CHURCH OF CHRIST

Farmington, Connecticut 1771

The work of gentlemen such as Peter Harrison and Joseph Brown was largely confined to the cities. However, they did have their rural counterparts, although the majority of these rural architect/builders remain unknown to us. Their buildings were an amalgam of ideas, some of which came from pattern-books and some of which they borrowed from other buildings in New England. They adapted these designs to the practical possibilities and limitations of building in the New England countryside. There is no better example of this architect/builder than Judah Woodruff of Farmington.

It was fitting that Farmington was home to a joiner of Woodruff's ability, as it was one of the largest and one of the most important of Connecticut's colonial communities. It was first settled in the early 1640s by people from Hartford. They were undoubtedly attracted by the fine farmland along the banks of the Tunxis River. Early meetings were held in people's houses, but there is evidence of a meetinghouse standing near the site of the present one by 1650. The First Church of Christ was formally organized in 1652. Farmington's link with Thomas Hooker's Hartford parish could hardly have been more direct; Farmington's first minister was Hooker's son-in-law, the second was his son. In her 1935 *History of Farmington,* Lydia Hewes gives a lively description of the role of the Farmington church:

> For nearly two hundred years the church was the active center of community life, and church dignitaries were the leaders in civic affairs. The meetinghouse was not only a place of prayer, but a place for town meetings, school exercises, and other occasions. For not attending church Seth North was known as "Sinner North," and court records show that fines were levied for non-attendance as well as for "giggling and laughing in church," and other misdemeanors with which the tithing-man could not cope.

> Until the foundation of other societies people came on foot and horseback from long distances, wives riding pillion behind their husbands. . . . There were sheds for horses, and "Sabbaday houses" near the church, where coals in foot-stoves could be replenished, in times before the church was heated, and where rest and comfort could be found when sermons and services were over-long.

The building of a second meetinghouse was proposed about 1709, but was not completed until 1714. It was built slightly north of the present meetinghouse, and had a pyramidal roof

77 The interior viewed from the gallery.

with a turret at the top. From that turret a drum was pounded to call the townspeople to meeting, though this was eventually replaced with a bell. There were three entrances and galleries. Within sixty years this building proved too small, and there are records of parishioners requesting permission to bring their chairs to meeting, presumably because the pews were full.

After much discussion the third—and present—Farmington meetinghouse was begun in the spring of 1771. Judah Woodruff was about fifty years old when he undertook the building of the meetinghouse. His ancestors were among the earliest settlers of Farmington.

78 The tower steps with the bell rope hanging at the right.

79 The main side entry door. The portico is an 1836 addition.

He had served in the French and Indian War as a lieutenant, and later held an officer's rank in the Continental Army. Between the two wars he built prolifically in Farmington, constructing about ten houses in addition to this meetinghouse. In his 1923 article, "From Meeting House to Church," Charles Place, minister at Lancaster, praised Woodruff's accomplishments:

> Built in 1771 by Captain Judah Woodruff of Farmington who is responsible for the design, the meeting house is remarkable for good proportions and the beauty of its spire. No finer example of the lines above the tower has been found outside of Boston. Evidence that Captain Woodruff ranked among the best of the good builders of the eighteenth century is found in the framing of the main structure and its tower. It is said that the sag in the ridge pole does not exceed two inches, and that the timbers of the tower today are almost plumb. A meeting house in plan it was in 1771 and is today, the interior showing still the old-time spirit, but though the three galleries remain, the old pews and original pulpit have disappeared ... President Porter in his centennial address says that Captain Woodruff carved with much care both the capitals of the pulpit and the vines ornamenting the sounding board; and it is a matter of keen regret that no description or illustration of these have been found.

Woodruff lavished the same care on the building of the meetinghouse that he did on the design, going to Boston to choose the finishing lumber himself, though the oak frame undoubtedly came from the forest around Farmington. The original split cedar roof shingles lasted 125 years, and the boards used to case the framework are not pitched, but rather unbroken lengths. As Place pointed out, Woodruff carved the pulpit and sounding-board himself; the historian Noah Potter has suggested that Woodruff often worked late into the night to complete this detailed work.

The basic form of the meetinghouse is quite straightforward. It is an oblong structure with the main entrance on the side and the high pulpit opposite. There is a tower at one end and a porch at the other. The deep three-sided gallery is supported by simple but graceful, turned columns. Tragically Woodruff's pulpit and sounding-board were removed in 1836 but, based on the little descriptive evidence available, a suitable attempt at a replacement has been made. The downstairs was originally planned with four square groups of box pews in the center, long pews at the side, and benches in the gallery. These gallery benches were removed in 1825 to 1826 and replaced with the present slip pews with doors. In 1836 the box pews downstairs were replaced. The small portico over the main entrance was added at this time as were shutters.

The spire is certainly the best-known feature of the meetinghouse. It is not known how the graceful framework was placed on top of the tower. It was long said that it was built on

80 A photograph taken *c.*1950, before the shutters were removed.

81 The interior: note the turned columns.

the ground and winched into place, though it seems more likely that somehow it was built *in situ*.

It is hard to say what the main influences were on Woodruff's design. The nearby Wethersfield meetinghouse was constructed just ten years before the Farmington church was begun, and was undoubtedly known to Woodruff. However, it is also interesting that the Wethersfield spire is a virtual duplication of the ones at Christ Church, Boston, and Trinity, Newport, whereas Woodruff's is a clear imitation of the spire of Old South, Boston. In fact, Woodruff may have made a spire slightly more graceful than its urban parent. There seems little reason to doubt that Woodruff saw his Farmington meetinghouse as a rural offspring of Old South. It also resembles the First Church meetinghouse which stood in Hartford at the time. Place ended his comments on Farmington thus:

> The influence of this meeting house must have been considerable in the whole Connecticut Valley, and the treatment of its spire is worthy of careful study, compared with earliest similar examples and succeeding designs in various parts of New England.

Regardless of its parentage, there is no question that Woodruff's Farmington meetinghouse spawned a brood of its own.

82 The façade, showing the delicate spire which is one of New England's finest.

THREE
MAINE MEETINGHOUSES

GERMAN MEETINGHOUSE
Waldoboro, Maine 1772

OLD WALPOLE MEETINGHOUSE
South Bristol, Maine 1772

ALNA MEETINGHOUSE
Alna, Maine 1789

Within about thirty miles of each other in Maine stand three meetinghouses remarkable not for any particularly rich individual history, but rather for their state of preservation, and for certain architectural features. In less rural areas they might well have disappeared, but this triumvirate north of Portland has remained pristine. The northernmost of them is the German Meetinghouse in Waldoboro, built in 1772.

The great migration of German Lutherans to America began in earnest around 1720. The bulk of them went to Pennsylvania and the southern colonies with a smattering of communities elsewhere. In the 1740s a group came to Waldoboro, which was probably their most northerly outpost. Though their location may seem isolated even today, they probably fared better than many of their compatriots who stayed nearer the towns and were often rather harshly exploited. This does not mean that life was easy. They named their settlement after General Samuel Waldo, proprietor of a Maine patent which included their territory in its vast acreage. He had encouraged the Germans' trek to the Northern coast. An inscription on a stone in the churchyard indicates that the settlers may have felt misled. It reads: "This town was settled in 1748 by Germans who migrated to this place with the promise and expectation of finding a prosperous city, instead of which they found nothing but a wilderness."

By 1773 they had carved a community out of that wilderness. It included two meetinghouses, one on the west side and the one we are concerned with here on the east side of the Medomak River. The building on the west side was the first to be completed but was soon judged to be too small. This, combined with the final settlement of various land-title disputes, led to the moving of the eastern meetinghouse. In the winter of 1795, when the

83 Waldoboro: the end porch entry.

84 Old Walpole: the end entry, shingled and shuttered.

85 Waldoboro: the gallery stairs, housed in the porch entry.

Mcdomak was frozen, the members skidded it across the ice and settled it on its present foundation. Coincidentally, this was the year the congregation received its first ordained minister, the Rev. Friedrich Augustus Rodolphus Benedictus Ritz, who is buried in the fine German churchyard which runs up the hill behind the church. He was followed in 1819 by Johannes Wilhelm Starman, the second and last ordained minister of this parish.

Language led to the parish's decline. The first generation spoke only German and insisted on holding services in the parent tongue. The second generation became bilingual, and the third fully adopted English. Despite its abandonment since then, the Old German Church, as it is often called, is still maintained by the local German Protestant Society, and services are held occasionally during the summer months.

From the outside the meetinghouse is a fairly standard form, with a simple pitched roof and a porch entry with a pedimented doorway. The porch, however, is on the end with the high pulpit opposite. This, of course, is not the traditional meetinghouse floor plan, which has the pulpit opposite a main entry on the long wall. The Lutherans clearly adopted a New England form for the exterior, but maintained a European church plan within. What inspired them to use a church form is uncertain. One clue may be that the interior was not completed

86 Old Walpole: the fine interior showing the marbleized pilasters.

87 Waldoboro: a view across the German burial ground.

in its present form until well after the chilly move over the Medomak ice. Overall, the interior is simple and handsome, with box pews below and a gallery above.

About fifteen miles southwest of Waldoboro at Christmas Cove stands the Old Walpole Meetinghouse in South Bristol. The first survey of the area named the town Walpole but early settlers renamed it Bristol in 1767. Though this meetinghouse was built five years after the change, it has retained the Walpole name. The parish was originally Presbyterian, probably because the first minister, Alexander McLain, was a Scottish Presbyterian who arrived in Bristol by way of New Jersey. The congregation was of necessity flexible about its sectarian affiliation. McLain served the parish from 1772 until 1800 when his assistant, a Congregationalist, took over. The parish's affiliation changed with its minister.

The interior has some unusual refinements for a rural meetinghouse. The high pulpit, in

88 Alna: looking back towards the entry.

89,90 Old Walpole: the main side entry; and the gallery stairs placed in the corner of the interior.

its traditional position opposite the main side entry, is detailed, with fluted marbleized pilasters leading up to the sounding-board. The gallery steps are in a corner as there is no porch to house them. In this respect, Walpole is more like Old St Paul's, Wickford, than Waldoboro and Alna. The exterior is straightforward except that it is shingled rather than clapboarded, and simple shutters are provided for most of the windows and all three entries. The shutters may very well date from post-1822 when regular services ceased. The doorways have simple pediments and pilasters. Local lore insists that the shingles are original, that when the meetinghouse was restored for its centennial they decided to leave the old ones because they were in good shape. Though this seems highly unlikely, the story is often repeated.

A few miles north of Christmas Cove is Alna, a town one might pass through without being aware of it except for its fine large meetinghouse and the old schoolhouse nearby. Though the meetinghouse has been called plain, it is "plain style" in the best Puritan sense. It was built in 1789 by a congregation that was large and thriving. Within fifty years of its construction it was being used sparingly at most, and ceased to have a regular minister, apparently because of parish confrontations and work migration. In 1889, as at Walpole, the townspeople celebrated the meetinghouse's centennial by restoring it.

We can be thankful that the Alna meetinghouse was restored: it is one of the finest of its

kind left in New England. From the moment one turns the old key in the door there is a sense that this is something special. The meetinghouse is painted yellow with green shutters and no one today can remember it being otherwise. There is a porch entry at the front with the pulpit opposite. The pulpit and sounding-board are carved and graceful, and the panelling throughout is painted or grained. The box pews are spindle-topped. The town continues to maintain this fine building, and there are occasional services in the summer.

Though there are meetinghouses of the general style and vintage of these three dotted around New England (Rockingham, Vermont, Sandown, New Hampshire, and Rocky Hill at Amesbury, Massachusetts, are three other excellent examples) one would be hard pressed to find another example of three buildings of such quality and in comparable states of preservation in such close proximity. It should be noted that the Harrington meetinghouse, another 1772 building in Bristol, has recently been restored as well.

92 The Alna meetinghouse.

91 Alna: the fine painted interior.

UNION CHURCH
AND OLD ST MARY'S

West Claremont, New Hampshire 1773 & 1823

There are times when the story of a given parish draws one to a building, in spite of its lack of overwhelming architectural appeal. West Claremont, New Hampshire, provides a clear example of this. The oldest Anglican church in the state, it stands almost directly across from the oldest Roman Catholic one, a fact that even the most casual observer would be hard pressed to chalk up to coincidence. In fact, the histories of the parishes are just as closely related as their proximity implies.

West Claremont is the part of the large township of Claremont which lies along the Connecticut River bank. It must have been settled about the time Benning Wentworth, New Hampshire's colonial governor, granted the land in 1764. The first of these two churches, built nine years after the grant, received its "Union" title apparently because its inception was a united effort of the region's Anglicans and Congregationalists. One of the tales of this unlikely combination involves an agreement which stipulated that the pastor should be a Congregationalist ordained in the Church of England. It is also said that Samuel Peters of Hebron, Connecticut, was involved in the founding of the parish. His was not likely to be a conciliatory voice as he was one of the most vocally "anti-Puritan" ministers in New England. At any rate, this seemingly convenient marriage was short-lived, breaking up, by most accounts, before the church was even completed, with Anglican rector Ranna Cossitt in charge.

Exactly when the church was "completed" is unclear, because of the Revolution; certainly the interior at Union Church was not completed until 1789. While there were many Tories in Claremont, there is no question that the Rev. Mr Cossitt and his flock suffered some persecution. There are records of Anglicans being jailed and forced to suffer punishments which, while not exactly cruel, were certainly humiliating. Cossitt himself left Claremont after the war.

Union is an attractive church, if not New England's most graceful. Its round-headed windows, squat cupola-topped belfry and expanse of clapboard are quite handsome. Originally it was only four bays long, and though the belfry was not added until 1801 there is no reason to assume that it was ever configured other than on the church plan. The main entry is through the tower. The last two bays at the other end were added in 1820, which is

clear from the exterior carpentry and the slightly different size of the windows. The interior has been changed but many of the earliest box pews are still present.

The theological problems at the birth of this parish were not its last. The next sectarian struggle began innocuously enough with the arrival of Daniel Barber as rector at Union in 1794. Barber had served on the loyalist side in the Revolution and, after his ordination by Bishop Seabury, was minister in the new Protestant Episcopal Church, first in upstate New York and then at Manchester, Vermont. He was Episcopal rector at Claremont for twenty-four years, serving the congregation "not liberally but with . . . scholarly wisdom." During these years Barber was increasingly drawn toward the Roman Catholic Church, becoming ever more convinced that his own Church had strayed.

In 1812, Barber made his first trip to Boston to meet with Roman Catholic authorities there and received books which gradually confirmed his leanings. He wrote in his memoirs:

> I had never seen a priest before. He treated me with great candor and gave me an understanding of the principal things that separate us from the Church of Rome. He also provided me with several books to carry home. . . . These few books scattered first among my Protestant neighbors. . . . In time some of the heads of the parish began to make complaints that these books I had lent among

96 Union Church: the box pews.

94 Union Church: note the entrance through the tower.
95 The two Claremont churches, with the back of Old St Mary's in the foreground.

97 Union Church: where the two sections join, as explained by a local.

98 Old St Mary's: a view before the parsonage fell down.

my parishioners were calculated to do harm . . . I put them under lock and key. But I soon found that by help of some of my children, they again found their way, more privately, abroad.

One of Barber's children played a particularly prominent part in his conversion. By 1815 Virgil Barber had followed his father into the Episcopal ministry. Together with his father and mother Virgil moved ever closer to Roman Catholicism. Cloë Barber was baptized a Roman in 1818. The same year Daniel left his ministry at Union and traveled south for a time. In 1822 Daniel and Virgil, now an ordained Roman priest (his wife became a nun), returned to their home across the street from Union Church. The next year Virgil built the brick church as an ell to their house which had been the Episcopal parsonage, which must have ruffled a few feathers in the valley.

The parsonage is now gone, but the Barbers' brick church, where Virgil also started the first Catholic school in New Hampshire, still stands. It is an odd but intriguing, tiny building, with a wide shallow tower and high narrow main structure. Its three levels include the church with a gallery in the rear, a schoolroom, and Virgil Barber's quarters above. The red-brick exterior has only the slightest ornamentation including indented pediments over the entry door and the tower and lower side windows. The tower has round windows at its uppermost level with urns and a simple cross above. Old St Mary's was replaced in 1870 by the present church near the center of Claremont, but the building is maintained and used for some seasonal services. Union Church stands almost directly across the street, and is still an active Episcopal congregation. In these more ecumenical times there is muted, almost charming, defiance in the scene.

FIRST BAPTIST CHURCH

Providence, Rhode Island 1775

In the winter of 1636 Roger Williams fled from Salem, in the Massachusetts Bay Colony, and moved gradually south, spending weeks in the wilderness. Eventually he fell into the hands of Indians, with whom he almost always maintained warm relations. Williams continued south to the head of Narragansett Bay where he purchased land from the Indians, also claimed by the colony from which Williams sought refuge. The settlement he founded there in 1636 became Providence. Together with Ezekiel Holliman, who had followed Williams from his Salem parish, he founded the colony's first church, now known as First Baptist Church.

In March 1639, Holliman and Williams baptized each other and ten other followers, thus establishing a Baptist congregation. With a typical display of irascible independence, Williams did not remain with the group for long. He could not accept the lack of apostolic administration in this new baptism. He withdrew from the church, his ministry and eventually from personal recognition of all church organization, though he never lost the knack for questioning their precepts. Despite Williams's actions, the American Baptist Church, and this parish in particular, proudly trace their roots to Williams and his vision of freedom of religion and conscience.

For the next sixty years the congregation worshipped in private homes, until, in 1700, Pardon Tillinghast, minister to the parish, built a small meetinghouse. One of the more remarkable aspects of the first building was its stove, which made it one of the earliest-heated houses of worship in New England. The first meetinghouse was replaced by a larger structure in 1721, but by 1774 the construction of a new building was being considered. Marguerite Appleton points out in her discussion of the church that it seems amazing that such an energetic enterprise should have been undertaken at a time when the winds of revolution were being whipped up throughout New England. She suggests a basic optimism in Providence as the explanation. Certainly, through the leadership of a lively commercial community, the town had prospered considerably since 1676 when the settlement had been almost levelled by the Indians during King Phillip's War. Enterprising merchants such as the four Brown brothers, Nicholas, Joseph, John and Moses, had positioned the town to take over the commercial reins of Rhode Island which Newport relinquished following the Revolution. The building of this remarkable meetinghouse affirms the confidence and the independent nature of this community, colony and congregation.

When the parish came to choose an architect, it turned to one of those very same brothers, Joseph Brown. He was Providence's answer to Newport's Peter Harrison. Like

99 The First Baptist Meetinghouse. Note the low tower entry.

100 A view of the meetinghouse in 1789.

Harrison, Brown was often called upon to undertake community architectural projects. When he began work on this meetinghouse, he had already designed the first college building at Rhode Island College (Brown) (1770), the Market House (1773), as well as his own home (1774). The house he designed for his brother John in 1786 is one of America's most famous and finest pieces of Federal architecture. The meetinghouse ranks as one of America's exemplary colonial buildings.

There are many points of architectural interest. In particular the Baptist church represents a transition from the meetinghouse to the church plan. Brown was certainly familiar with Boston's houses of worship and was thoroughly conversant with contemporary church and meetinghouse designs. In fact, the design committee, composed of Brown, Jonathan Hammond and Comfort Wheaton, was sent to Boston to look at churches and meetinghouses there. The solution they arrived at was an intriguing compromise. The building was originally intended to be oblong, measuring 90 by 70 feet, but was changed to a square, 80 by 80 feet, in the final design, a clear throwback to the earliest of New England's meetinghouses. The placement of the entrances is of particular interest. The porch at the tower end has an entrance and the high pulpit was placed on the same axis across from it.

101 The interior after restoration.

102 Three designs for a spire by James Gibbs: it is the one in the center that Joseph Brown followed most closely.

103 The interior before the restoration: note the pulpit recess and the decorative painting on the ceiling.

This assimilation of the church plan was countered by central entrances on both the remaining sides, in deference to the meetinghouse form. The layout of the original box pews, which are now gone, supports the notion that these side entrances were probably of equal stature to the main one.

The most stunning feature of the church is its steeple. Nowhere in New England is the direct influence of eighteenth-century English design more apparent. This time the source of the design can be directly traced. Brown's fondness for James Gibbs's *Book of Architecture* (1728) is unquestioned, and here he has definitely drawn his design from one of the proposed, but rejected, spires for Gibbs's St Martin-in-the-Fields in London. Brown made only minor adjustments to Gibbs's design. There are three main stages. The lowest is an open-arched belfry and above it two octagonal stages with round-headed windows. The only substantive change to the design is the upper octagonal stage which Gibbs had sketched as cylindrical. In his exhaustive study of the building, Norman Isham grapples with the questions raised by the herculean task of constructing this tall tower. He concludes that the various wooden stages must have been built from within the tower. The tower and each successive stage of the steeple therefore was able to act as support for block and tackle to lift the rest, and no massive outside scaffolding was necessary. The rest of the exterior is equally compelling. The tower rests on a deep narrow porch with a palladian window above the central entry. There are strong corner quoins, dentiled cornices, and framed round-headed windows all around the building. The tower entrance is, in fact, much lower than the side ones, largely because of the land's steep slope.

The interior has a large central barrel-vaulted ceiling with groined arches above the galleries. The columns run from floor to ceiling, supporting the side arches and the gallery. The rear gallery was altered in 1834 to accommodate the organ, which still has its 1834 case. The box pews were replaced by slip pews in 1832 and the high pulpit was replaced by a platform with a recess chancel in 1884. A major restoration in the late 1950s left the pews but restored the pulpit wall. The detail, while not as elaborate as Harrison's King's Chapel, Boston, is excellent, with fluted columns and pilasters, fine panelling, urns and scrolled broken-pedimented doorways (similar to Brown's later work on his brother's house). Arched keystone architraves on the pulpit wall windows mirror the detailing on the exterior windows and on the arch over the reinstated pulpit, pulpit window and sounding-board. The Waterford crystal chandelier was given by Hope Brown, daughter of Nicholas, in 1792, and was first lit on the evening of her marriage to Thomas Poynton Ives.

This meetinghouse stands at a pivotal point in New England's architectural history. It is a colonial building poised at the edge of the Federal style. In its design it reaches back to the colonial meetinghouse, draws its most remarkable features from English design, and looks ahead to the emergence of a definitively American Federal architecture.

104 Detail of a carved scrolled broken-pedimented doorway.
105 The gallery: note the fine arches and dosserets above the capitals.

OLD MEETINGHOUSE

Rockingham, Vermont 1787

Religion came to Rockingham long before the first settlers put down roots there. On March 5th, 1704, John Williams, captive minister of Deerfield, Massachusetts, held services at the mouth of the river which would later bear his name. Just one week after the raid on frontier Deerfield a tired and lame ("having before my travel wronged my ankle bone and sinews") Williams stood on the banks of the Connecticut and preached to his hundred and twelve fellow captives. His description of the scene comes from his journal entitled *The Redeemed Captive*:

> On the Saturday the journey was long and tedious; We traveled with such speed that four women were tired and then slain by them who laid them captive. On the Sabbath day we rested, and I was permitted to pray and preach to the captives. The place of the Scripture spoken from was Lam: I:18: "The Lord is righteous, for I have rebelled against his commandment. Hear, I pray you, all people, and behold my sorrow. My virgins and my young men have gone into captivity."

The land around the Williams river must have seemed less threatening fifty years later when Rockingham was first settled, and positively cosmopolitan when the first meetinghouse was raised in 1774. The legend of the siting of this first meetinghouse is typical, and apparently indicative of the kind of trouble this parish was prone to. Two sites were suggested, one where the present building stands, and another—now unknown—site, presumably further south and less pleasing to Rockingham residents. The southern site was chosen in an open meeting, but the night before construction was to begin some of the irate minority removed all the building materials to their preferred site, and the first meetinghouse was erected, after a hasty meeting the next morning, at the place now known as Meetinghouse Hill.

That first meetinghouse was apparently a small one, because by 1786 the community determined that it needed a larger building. The exact date of the raising of this new meetinghouse on the old site is uncertain, but the best evidence seems to point toward June 9th, 1787. This account of General Fuller, a leading resident who apparently oversaw the construction, comes from a late nineteenth-century Rockingham descendant:

> After he got everything ready the old General (Fuller) took his bottle of rum in one hand, a tumbler in the other and stood on the plate of the last of the south

106 The façade and one of the two porch entries.

107 The interior, showing the box pews and benches.

side, then gave the order to put it up in that position. He rode up on the plate, and he was a man weighing 200 pounds. When they had got it up, he stood on the plate, drank his health to the crowd below, then threw his bottle and tumbler down and called for the ladder, coming down amid loud and long cheering.

The town had difficulty completing the structure. It was first used for town meetings in 1792 at which point the interior was still far from completion. People sat on pews constructed of logs with rough boards laid across them. Arrangements were made in 1793 to sell the first meetinghouse which stood nearby on the hill, and yet by all accounts the interior of the new house was not finished until 1801—fourteen years after the frame was raised.

Such a tentative, even uncertain, approach to religious affairs is typical of this parish. From 1773 to 1839 the congregation slipped in and out of organization, with its only truly energetic period being between 1773 and 1809. During this time it remained under the stewardship of one pastor, the Rev. Samuel Whiting. He was apparently a warm, liberal-minded and probably long-suffering individual who attended services at the church after his retirement regardless of what sect's views were being promulgated. He was quoted as saying that "they may be right and I wrong." During his pastorate his pay was often as much as a year in arrears, a fact about which he was apparently capable of good humor. A parishioner once castigated him by commenting that of late they had received "poor preaching, very poor preaching," to which Whiting replied: "You must not forget that I receive poor pay, very poor pay."

After 1839 the building ceased to be regularly used for religious gatherings, but continued to serve for Town Meetings until after the Civil War. After 1869, however, the building became dilapidated. The interior was a treasure trove for memento hunters who particularly seemed to enjoy removing the spindles from the box pew rails and the hand-forged hinges from the pew doors. The lack of use had its positive aspect: despite some depradations and the alteration of the pulpit in 1851, the interior remained virtually unchanged.

In 1906 the restoration of the meetinghouse was undertaken as the result of the appropriation of $500 of town funds. The building was overhauled from top to bottom. The foundations were restored and the slate roof replaced. Sixty pew doors had to be reconstructed; and over 1400 spindles in the pew rails needed replacing as only two original ones remained. Stoves were removed, pew-door hinges replicated, and the pulpit was restored in as accurate a fashion as possible.

The result is stunning. Rockingham meetinghouse is a classic, with porches east and west housing the gallery stairs, a main entrance to one side and the high pulpit opposite, and a gallery on three walls. Ironically, we can thank the awkward location of the building, the

108 An early annual pilgrimage to the meetinghouse. These began in 1907.

109 An early photograph of the interior, showing the stove-pipes which provided a typical system of heating.

110 Detail of the pulpit and sounding-board.

111 The back of the meetinghouse from across the burial ground. Note the pulpit window in the center of the back wall.

tentative nature of the parish and the energetic preservationism of a group of early twentieth-century Vermonters for the building's few changes and remarkable condition. No belltower or steeple was ever added and the box pews were never replaced.

Though the restoration was completed in 1906, the rededication of the building was delayed until the summer of 1907 in order to enable descendants and other interested people to attend. Nearly 1200 people attended this Old Home Day and a pilgrimage of a similar nature has become an annual event. In 1911, the Old Rockingham Meeting House Association was established to preserve this and other buildings of importance. The meetinghouse is open to the public on a seasonal basis.

In addition to its historical and architectural importance, the location of the church is spectacular. It overlooks the valley through which the river runs where John Williams preached. All round is an ancient cemetery which contains many of the graves of the founders of the church and is one of the finest in New England. The Rockingham meetinghouse is a building which really does have to be "seen to be believed."

SABBATHDAY LAKE SHAKER MEETINGHOUSE

New Gloucester, Maine 1794

At the height of the Shaker movement, in the nineteenth century, there were eighteen communities in America. None of them survives today except as a museum, where the buildings and artifacts have been carefully maintained. The Shakers are now best known for their simple, elegant, and consummately practical furniture, and other crafts. In addition, the communities consistently produced innovations such as the clothes peg, the flat broom, the circular saw and the automatic spring. Some of their buildings, however, are equally memorable, and have the same simplicity, elegance and functionality.

The sect's roots lie in a French seventeenth-century revival embraced by a group called the Camisards, who probably spread their religious fervor to England. There, though it did not find widespread success, it was adopted by some Quakers who believed in highly energetic physical expressions of religious awakening and feeling. As the Quaker movement

112 Traditional Shaker furniture in the upper rooms of the meetinghouse.

113 The main meeting-room.

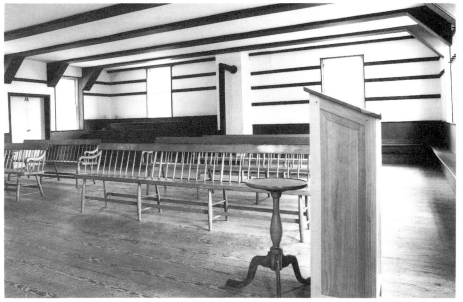

114 The meetinghouse viewed from the south.

had grown out of the left wing of English Puritanism, the Shaking Quakers, as they were sometimes called, separated themselves from the Quakers by a "further degree of light and power." In 1747, Jane and James Wardley formed a society in Manchester, England. Among their small band of converts was Ann Lee, destined to become the great Shaker prophet. Mother Ann, as she came to be called, was the daughter of a blacksmith and married, at a very early age, another. She had had a difficult youth and came to the Wardleys uneducated and illiterate. She professed a lifelong struggle for religious revelation which culminated with her conversion. She took to the Shaker vision of physical exaltation with uncommon zeal, and soon outshone all her fellows. Her fellow Shakers began to believe Mother Ann to be the Second Coming of Christ, a female counterpart to Jesus who would take a place in the Shaker Trinity. Her trances and visions grew ever more intense and in time she too began to believe in her role. She produced four children, all of whom died young, and her marriage did not survive her deification. She became convinced that sexual relations had, since Adam and Eve, been at the root of human sinfulness. England in the 1770s was not a congenial place to

115 A rear view of the tiny gambrel-roofed meetinghouse.

promulgate theories about the female embodiment of Christ's Second Coming, and the band, and Mother Ann in particular, was persecuted. In 1774, Mother Ann and eight followers traveled to America.

Persecution aside, poverty had dogged the Shakers in England, and the problem stayed with them once across the ocean. The notion of communal living, which had previously played no part in Shaker philosophy, now became an integral part of Shaker life. The group, first settled at New Lebanon near Albany, New York, had success wherever and whenever religious revivalism flourished, attracting those who felt the spirit move within them most energetically. Late eighteenth-century New England provided fertile ground, and the sect continued to grow, even after Mother Ann's death in 1784. By 1794 there were twelve communities, two in New York and the rest in New England: four in Massachusetts, two in New Hampshire, one in Connecticut and three in the District of Maine. The three in Maine were at Alfred, Gorham and New Gloucester.

The New Gloucester community was organized in April 1794 near Sabbathday Pond. Two years earlier, three Shaker preachers had come north from Gorham and had gradually gained enough converts to support a community. The first order of business was to build a meetinghouse and a community dwelling house. The dwelling house was a massive four-story clapboarded structure with a large, enclosed porch. In striking contrast, the meetinghouse, which was actually built first, sat across the road. It is a small building, which represents the best in Shaker simplicity. It has been little changed, though the rooms in the upper two stories are now part of the museum. The timber had been confidently cut, presumably by the Gorham preachers, two years before. The meetinghouse was raised on June 14th, 1794 and it was completed for Christmas.

It is a tiny gambrel-roofed building, clapboarded, with three gables on each side. There are chimneys at each end, each made of 10,000 small bricks produced by the community, who also made all their own nails. There are two front entry doors. In 1839 a small ell was added at the north end of the meetinghouse and the stairway was moved into it. The two stories above the meeting-room originally housed the Shaker Maine Ministry, which served the communities at Alfred and New Gloucester. The interior meeting-room is stark but graceful, the only adornments being some paint, a few pews and wall benches, the furniture and the twelve long beams which run across the width of the building.

The original dwelling place was completed in 1795, but a massive brick replacement was built in 1883. Various other buildings were raised during the nineteenth century, including an Herb House, dairy barns, stables, the Spin House, the Laundry, and the Great Mill.

Industry at New Gloucester was remarkably diverse, ranging from farming, apple orchards, saw, grist and woolen mills, the manufacture of wooden ware such as tubs, pails, chairs and oval boxes, to the sale of garden seeds. The community thrived during the nineteenth century, but has since declined. The meetinghouse is still in use, however, and the museum is open to the public between May and September.

FIRST RELIGIOUS SOCIETY

Newburyport, Massachusetts 1800

Newbury, north of Boston, was one of the numerous Puritan settlements during the 1630s, the critical decade of migration. The town was first settled in 1635 and grew so quickly that it gave rise to two others, West Newbury and Newburyport. As with other coastal communities, commercial talents were mainly concerned with the sea, first with small fishing vessels and later with large wharves accommodating all manner of trade and finally with shipbuilding. With the growth of the town came the inevitable religious complications. The people who had settled inland of the original landfall soon began to clamor for an independent parish, a possibility which carried more ramifications than just the building of a new meetinghouse. The parish organization was the central cog in local government and commerce and the original parish was often reluctant to surrender a portion of its power base. Newbury's First Parish went so far as to move the original meetinghouse two miles closer to its western settlers in an attempt to defuse the threatened explosion. The westerners, however, had clearly decided that compromise was unsatisfactory. In 1694, the Second Parish was established and it eventually became West Newbury.

To the northwest of the town of Newbury, near the mouth of the Merrimack, a new settlement sprouted, which came to be appropriately known as the Newtown section of Newbury. It was here that commerce really began to thrive, and it was inevitable that these settlers would also petition for independence from the older, less active First Parish at Newbury. It was equally inevitable that the request would receive a frosty response. In 1722, however, the First Parish acceded and the Third Parish of Newbury was formed. In 1764 the Third Parish became the present Newburyport. The parish, then Congregational, now Unitarian, became the First Religious Society.

The First Newtown meetinghouse was built in 1725 and one observer felt it was so close to the First Parish "that I fear that it will make a great contention." This first building was oblong, 45 by 60 feet, with "the steeple fronting the river." The mention of a steeple at this date is something of a surprise, but we can be certain there was one by 1754 as the spire was struck by lightning and had to be rebuilt. One interested observer of the damage was Benjamin Franklin:

> In my late journey I saw an instance of a great quantity of lightning, conducted by
> a wire no bigger than a common knitting needle. It was at Newbury, in New
> England, where the spire of the church steeple, being 70 feet above the belfry,

was split all to pieces, and thrown about the streets in fragments, from the bell down to the clock, placed in the steeple, 20 feet below the bell, there was a small wire . . . which connected the motion of the clock to the hammer striking the hour on the bell . . . The clock wire was blown all to smoke, and smutted the church wall, which passed in a broad, black tract, and also the ceiling under which it was carried.

The first meetinghouse was enlarged in 1764. Then, in 1785, just over twenty years after Newburyport's incorporation as an independent town, the congregation began to consider replacing the old house. By the late 1790s land had been procured and construction began in 1800. It took more than a year and the new meetinghouse was not dedicated until October 2, 1801. It cost $26,750.01. The building committee left no doubt that they desired a prominent structure, "with a cellar, a Portico or piazza and a handsome Belfry or Spire."

Unfortunately, the committee did leave us in doubt as to the architect of the building. They certainly commissioned specific plans, but who penned them remains a mystery. For

116 , 117 The elegant meetinghouse.

118 The pulpit.

119 Detail of a capital on the pulpit wall.

many years the most likely person was assumed to be Timothy Palmer. He was known to have remarkable mechanical skills and, like Captain Isaac Damon (who designed a number of churches including the one at Springfield, Massachusetts), he was a noted bridge-builder. Palmer's brother ran the construction firm of Palmer and Spofford. However, this attribution is slightly suspect. Whoever built the Newburyport meetinghouse had a talent for detail and fine carving that rivalled any New England architect of the period. The turn of the century was the time of Samuel McIntire's best work in nearby Salem, and his influence is evident here. The detail in the pulpit at Newburyport is particularly reminiscent of McIntire, with its finely carved swags, baskets of fruit, and foliate capitals. It is hard to believe that McIntire could have been so near and not have been involved. Unfortunately, his 1803 Salem church, said to resemble this one in many respects, is gone.

The committee's request for a "handsome Belfry or Spire" received a positive response. Though there are elements of Christ Church, Boston, in the top of the tower, the fine steeple is clearly the coastal precursor of the less ornate, rural steeples inspired by Elias Carter's church at Templeton. The Newburyport steeple rises in three stages. The first is an open-arched belfry, while the top two are octagonal, the lower with round-headed windows and the upper with pointed windows. The three stages are topped by a spire. The detail in the steeple is remarkable. The tower and lower two stages have dentiled cornices and decorated friezes. The belfry stage is adorned with pilasters and the open arches are framed by columns, topped by a keystone arch. The second-stage cornice is supported by freestanding Corinthian columns and is topped by urns. The tower rests on a fine, pedimented porch with central and corner pilasters. There are three entries, all with pilasters; the outer entries have finely carved lintels, while the central one has a broken pediment surmounting a fanlight. The outer windows above the entries are round-headed with arches which match those in the belfry, while the central window is palladian. The carving in the arch over the curve in the palladian window matches that over the central doorway. The same kind of care has been lavished on the interior, with particular attention having been paid to the magnificent pulpit wall. Here most of the exterior motifs are repeated, often with even more detail. This is indicative of the overwhelming attraction of this building which is one of coherent vision, detailed but not busy, and full of light and air.

120 A detail of the frieze on the pulpit.

THE CHURCH ON THE HILL

Lenox, Massachusetts 1805

The transition from meetinghouse to church is without question the most important development in New England's ecclesiastical architecture. The early urban examples of the church plan were due to wealthy Anglicans who looked back to their English roots with pride and who desired to emulate English church architecture. The adoption of this design in rural, and overwhelmingly Congregational, areas, however, was a breakthrough which permanently changed the face of the New England town green. The Church on the Hill at Lenox is a good example of the change that occurred.

The change in style can be dated quite definitely to the building of two church-plan meetinghouses in 1789, one in Taunton, Massachusetts, and one in Pittsfield, Massachusetts. There were, of course, a number of developments before the major change occurred, such as the addition of belltowers, the eventual placement of the entrance through the towers, and the rearrangement of the interiors. Peter Benes points towards specific changes in rural architecture such as the belltower built at Guilford, Connecticut, in 1726, which was probably inspired by the tower at Trinity, Newport. In Pittsfield, however, a coherent and dramatically new overall design emerged, with Charles Bulfinch as the architect.

The Pittsfield meetinghouse was not only revolutionary in its interior layout. Bulfinch also incorporated the tower by making it the center of the pedimented porch with a cupola belfry above. This new porch design included the main entrance to the church-plan building. Bulfinch may have seen various buildings which inspired him, among them Providence's First Baptist meetinghouse. At Providence, however, despite the incorporated tower, there are still prominent side entrances. These have disappeared in the Bulfinch design. Bulfinch also drew on buildings such as King's Chapel and Thomas Dawes' Brattle Street Church, Boston, as well as on certain European buildings.

The Pittsfield meetinghouse is gone but it left its mark on the area. The style was mimicked in various towns including Richmond, Massachusetts (1794), Salisbury, Connecticut (1798), Lee, Massachusetts (1800), and at Lenox in 1805. In 1797, a design, similar to that of Bulfinch for Pittsfield, was published in Asher Benjamin's great American design-book, *The Country Builder's Assistant.* The local dissemination of church architectural styles will receive closer examination in the section on Elias Carter's building in Templeton, Massachusetts. For the moment, let it suffice to say that instances of such neighborly architectural borrowing in New England are legion and Lenox gives us an excellent example, particularly because of its probable relationship to Bulfinch's Pittsfield church.

In 1805, the congregation at Lenox voted to build a new meetinghouse. The contract stated that "the steeple and the workmanship of it (was) to be made conformable to the plan of the steeple laid down in . . . Benjamin's *Country Builder's Assistant.*" What they received was a combination of the Bulfinch and Benjamin designs. The porch, for instance, has a central entry door and window typical of the Bulfinch design rather than of Benjamin, and the palladian windows on the tower, two of which were replaced by the present clock, are also typical of Bulfinch. The explanation for the deviation from the contract's stipulations seems clear: the congregation hired a builder named Benjamin D. Goodrich of Richmond, Massachusetts, who incorporated elements of his home town church in the design for Lenox. The handsome church and its cemetery are magnificently sited overlooking the town.

The interior of the Lenox church has been much changed. The box pews were replaced in 1840. The floorplan was altered at this time as well, and the pulpit and gallery front were both lowered. The major structural change came in 1880, when the pulpit wall was pushed back and the present curved chancel, platform and round window were installed. The organ dates from 1868.

Lenox stands in an area first settled in the mid-eighteenth century, a rugged territory in the heart of the Berkshire hills of western Massachusetts. It was originally known by the Indian name, Yokontown, but was officially incorporated as Lenox in 1767. One hundred years later this hilltop community was on the verge of major change. The still relatively

121 The interior, showing the late 19th-century extension of the pulpit wall.

122 The interior viewed from the chancel.

isolated town became a summer haven for well-heeled city dwellers who built "cottages" of size and architectural interest. Lenox became a Newport in the Berkshires.

The early history of the parish was dominated by one pastor, Samuel Shepard, who oversaw the building of the present meetinghouse and served his congregation for more than half a century. Two descriptions of him are notable. The first comes from a later pastor, Dr R. DeWitt Mallary, in his book *Lenox and the Berkshire Highlands* (1902), and the second is a childhood eyewitness account from William Bartlett's *Half Century Memories*:

> Samuel Shephard was called to the pastorate of the village Congregational church when a mere boy just out of Yale Callege, where he graduated in 1793. He died with the harness on, having ministered continuously in the same place for fifty years and a few months. He was installed at an open-air service just outside the church door; his grave is near the identical spot of ground where that service was held, and is surmounted with a monument on which is this appropriate verse: "Remember the words which I spake unto you while I was yet with you." The village is filled with the story of this man, who lived to baptize the great-grandchildren of his first converts, and who saw the promise of the Lord to "his children, and their seed and their seed's seed" fulfilled. He witnessed ten "special manifestations of the divine influence, or revivals" during which scores and even hundreds were gathered into the church. He was a man of cheerful, sunny temperament and social qualifications, somewhat different from the prevailing type of the clergy of the period. An earnest preacher with a peculiarly deep, sonorous voice, his sermons were listened to with more than formal attention.

> How plainly I can see Dr Shepard ascending the long flight of steps to the pulpit; how grand and solemn to hear his sonorous and melodious voice fill the high arched room as he began the service and continued it in reading the hymn, as he only could! How his praying with his eyes apparently open (owing to an infirmity of his eyelids) kept the roguish boys in check!

The Lenox area also has a rich literary tradition which stretches back to Jonathan Edwards's ministry to the Indians in nearby Stockbridge. His eight-year residence there began in 1750, following his dismissal from Northampton, and was his most prolific time. Other writers found success—and refuge—in the Berkshire hills around Lenox, including Nathaniel Hawthorne, Oliver Wendell Holmes, Harriet Beecher Stowe, Henry Ward Beecher and Edith Wharton. The British actress Fanny Kemble fell in love with Lenox, and owned property there. In her *Records of Later Life* she wrote longingly from London in 1845, with a drawing of Lenox before her: "I believe I do like places better than people."

123 The Church on the Hill in winter.

THE OLD FIRST CHURCH

Old Bennington, Vermont 1805

The following advertisement appeared in the *Vermont Gazette* of February 14th, 1804:

> Proposals will be received by the undersigned for the framing of a meeting-house 70x52 ft. with porch, cupola, and tower agreeable to a draft or plan to be at all seasonable hours exhibited to any person wishing to give their proposals. Said proposals must include the necessary superintendence of the master-workman and his assistants in putting the frame up, complete fit for covering, to be done and prepared by the 15th of June next. It is understood that all materials necessary for erecting and finishing the said building will be delivered on the spot.
>
> *Moses Robinson Jr.*

The plans which the distinguished Governor Robinson "exhibited to any appropriate contractor" were exceptional. They came from the hand of Lavius Fillmore, an architect

124 The original meetinghouse, built in 1763.

125 The interior, *c.*1910.

126 The interior viewed from the pulpit.

who, in his limited production, displayed possibly as artful a style as any New England church builder. His two Vermont churches are his masterpieces.

It is fitting that the hill, now Old Bennington, should be graced with such a building. The first meetinghouse, the parish and the town feature prominently in the history of the state and the country. The town of Bennington was granted a charter in 1749 by New Hampshire's Colonial Governor Benning Wentworth, but because of the French and Indian Wars it was not settled before 1761. The settlers came from Hardwick, Massachusetts, and were in the vanguard of a migration to Vermont which saw the population grow from about 300 in 1760 to 85,425 in 1790. Bennington was the first Vermont settlement west of the Green Mountains, had the oldest charter of any town, built the first meetinghouse in the territory, and in 1762 formed the Church of Christ which was the earliest parish gathered in Vermont.

The first meetinghouse, which was completed before 1766, was built in the oblong colonial style. It stood on the green in Old Bennington and played a crucial role in episodes of Vermont history. The meetinghouse was used as a courtroom, served as a hospital during the Battle of Bennington, and was the seat of eight sessions of the Vermont legislature, including the one which saw the ratification of the United States Constitution. The Rev. Jedidiah Dewey was the community's earliest minister. While giving thanks in the old

127 The interior showing the restored pulpit wall and box pews. Note the ceiling dome with the cross around it.

meetinghouse for Ethan Allen and his Green Mountain Boys' victory at Ticonderoga, Dewey had to put up with Allen leaping to his feet and demanding, in typically egocentric fashion, that he get equal billing with God.

By the 1790s Bennington's population had grown to more than 2000 and had outgrown the old meetinghouse. Discussions concerning a new building began as early as 1792, but one can see from the advertisement quoted above that it was not until 1804 that construction actually began. The site chosen was just south of the old meetinghouse on the green.

Lavius (a cousin of the more famous though possibly less deserving Millard) Fillmore was born in Norwich, Connecticut, in 1767, but had settled in Middlebury, Vermont, by 1806. Fillmore built the churches in Norwichtown (1801) and East Haddam (1794), Connecticut; and it is clear from both that his distinctive style, apparently derived from the great eighteenth-century design-books, was already well developed. The exteriors of both Connecticut churches bear the mark of Fillmore's later work, particularly in their strong façades which feature pedimented entries, dentiled cornices, round-topped upper windows and massive corner quoins. Glenn Andres, in his Dublin Seminar paper on Fillmore, raises some difficult questions over the design of the interior of the East Haddam church. The interior is similar to

128,129 The Bennington meetinghouse in winter and in summer.

130 The view from the rear gallery: note the curve in the gallery railing and the groined arches above.

Bennington, but has features which are not typical of provincial New England architecture of the date—features which were still very new even in Boston, having just been introduced by Charles Bulfinch. More will need to be discovered about Fillmore's youth before we can ascertain how this rural twenty-four-year-old came to employ such a sophisticated design.

Fillmore's two Vermont churches at Bennington and Middlebury (completed 1809) are his finest. Many would call Middlebury the better of the two. Certainly the steeple at Middlebury is one of the finest in New England. The interior of the Middlebury church, however, has been altered while that at Bennington has been lovingly restored. Its present condition, and its site, confirms its standing as one of the most beautiful churches in New England.

The palladian window over the central entry door at Bennington is an addition to his Connecticut façade. Fillmore also employed the palladian window at Middlebury, though the pediment over the window is broken at Bennington and not at Middlebury. The Bennington church is the only example of Fillmore's work where he used palladian windows in the lowest stage of the steeple. In Middlebury he reverted to the round-topped window of his Connecticut days. The belfry at Bennington is a squat, octagonal two-stage structure, open at the lower stage and closed above. It is topped by an ogee dome.

The interior is extremely elegant. The curve of the central ceiling dome is reflected in the back of the gallery, the round-topped windows and the fine groined arches over the windows and in the corners. Columns with leafed capitals run from the floor to the ceiling and were each hewn from single pine timbers. The palladian pulpit window overlooks the relatively simple high pulpit and neat rows of restored box pews.

It is hard to believe now but during the nineteenth century, as was often the case, the parish determined that they could improve on the interior. They went about it with a vengeance. The boxes were replaced by slip pews, and the high pulpit was replaced with the everpresent platform, the panels of the fine clear palladian window were covered with stained glass and an arched enclosure added in the chancel. In a number of churches the nineteenth-century modifications are intriguing and even occasionally pleasing, but in the case of a building as handsome as this one the restoration of its early nineteenth-century interior was essential.

Thanks to the efforts of Dr Vincent Ravi-Booth (pastor of the church from 1919 to 1944 and founder of Bennington College), in 1936 and 1937 the church was restored and the clean elegance of Fillmore's vision finally reappeared.

The beautiful cemetery which fans out behind the church is probably Vermont's most historic and certainly one of its most beautiful. The graves include those of both the British and American dead from the Battle of Bennington, five Vermont Governors, the famed Vermont printer and founder of the *Vermont Gazette* Anthony Haswell, and the poet Robert Frost. Some stones were apparently moved when the church was built. The churchyard represents an important chapter in the history of this gateway town of Vermont. Dr Ravi-Booth referred to the yard as "Vermont's sacred acre," and Fillmore's church as its "Westminster Abbey." A trifle grand perhaps, but not far from the mark.

THOMAS HOOKER'S
HARTFORD DESCENDANTS

FIRST CHURCH OF CHRIST
Hartford, Connecticut 1806

SECOND CHURCH OF CHRIST
Hartford, Connecticut 1826

131 The Center Church meetinghouse, home of the First Church of Hartford.

132,133 The South meetinghouse, home of the Second Church of Hartford: exterior and detail of the steeple.

136

The names of the leading religious lights of New England's first two generations—including Roger Williams, Cotton and Increase Mather or even John Cotton—are known to many Americans. Thomas Hooker is less well known, and yet his contribution was as dramatic. Cotton Mather described Hooker, who went into the wilderness and established Hartford, as "the light of the western churches." Some historians believe that it was Hooker's independence which established the separate nature of Connecticut's Congregational church, which in turn was largely responsible for its subsequent success.

Hooker was born in Marfield, England, in 1586. Little is known of his earliest years except that he went to Cambridge in 1604. Emmanuel College, which he attended, was a hotbed of Puritanism. He completed two degrees and remained there as a resident fellow, preaching and teaching occasionally. In 1620 he was called as rector to a small parish in Surrey, and later went to St Mary's in Chelmsford as a lecturer. The role of lecturer in a seventeenth-century English parish was complicated, but basically it was a way to support a Puritan voice in a community while attempting to circumvent the ire of the Church of England. The success of this arrangement was often only limited, particularly when the preacher was an accomplished one. Though Hooker received energetic local support, he also acquired the enmity of Archbishop Laud. He was called to appear before the High Commission Court, but instead went to Holland.

Holland was often a staging post for expatriate English Puritans, and Hooker was no exception. His loyal Chelmsford audience communicated their desire to have him lead them to New England. Confident, they traveled on ahead to Boston, settling in Newtown (Cambridge) in 1632. Though they were known as "Mr Hooker's company," he did not actually join them until the next year. Hooker spoke for many a Puritan emigré and with typical Puritan certainty, when he said in his farewell sermon at Chelmsford:

> England has seen her best dayes, and now evill dayes are befalling us . . . God
> is packing up his Gospel, because no body will buy his wares, nor come to his
> price . . .

Hooker came across on the same ship as John Cotton, who became minister at Boston. He did not remain in Massachusetts long. The exact cause of the congregation's migration to Connecticut in 1636 is uncertain, but it seems probable that by then Hooker recognized that the only way he could truly speak freely and without undue doctrinal confrontation was by escaping the already somewhat confining nature of Massachusetts' Puritanism. The Bay Colony proved too small to hold both Hooker and Cotton. Ola Winslow wondered if Hooker found "life in the orbit of John Cotton was less free than his nature and powers demanded? Did one walk a chalk line even here?" The General Court at first refused Hooker's request to move to the Connecticut Valley, but persistence prevailed.

Hooker was about fifty when he undertook the two-week journey to Connecticut with his flock. Benjamin Trumbull described the trek in his 1797 *Complete History of Connecticut, Civil and Ecclesiastical*:

134 The gallery rails and ceiling at Second Church.

> They had no guide but their compass; made their way over mountains, thro'
> swamps, thickets and rivers, which were not passable but with great difficulty.
> They had no cover by the heavens, nor any lodging but that which simple nature
> afforded them. They drove with them a hundred and sixty cattle, and by the
> way, subsisted on the milk of their cows. The people generally carried their
> packs, arms and some utensils. This adventure was the more remarkable, as
> many of this company were persons of figure, who had lived, in England, in
> honor, affluence and delicacy, and were entire strangers to fatigue and danger.

When they arrived they found a small, fledgling community. Hooker spent the last eleven years of his life in Hartford, though he returned to Boston on a number of occasions for gatherings and synods, including the synod which considered the case of Anne Hutchinson. The highlight of his years in Connecticut was his role in the writing of the Fundamental Orders, which provided a constitutional framework for the Connecticut Valley towns.

Thomas Hooker was a complex man. His westward migration was inspired by a thirst for both independence and land. Some have argued that Hooker energetically enunciated democratic principles long before his Massachusetts counterparts. His outline for a sermon he delivered in 1638 includes some startling clauses concerning government by universal suffrage, rule of the "people," setting limits to government power and the writing of laws; he also had a comparatively liberal attitude toward the issue of church membership, and questioned the Puritan ideal of "visible saints" long before the adoption of the Half-Way Covenant. On the other hand, when Hooker talked about "people," he certainly meant church members not "just folks," and felt that excess debate would "doubtless break the church in pieces." Hooker's very presence in Connecticut gave the colony a position and voice that it might not otherwise have gained as rapidly, while he remained an articulate spokesman for the New England Way and the traditional precepts of Congregationalism.

The First and Second Churches of Christ stand a few blocks from each other in downtown Hartford. They are both direct descendants of Hooker's first parish. Though the building of these two meetinghouses was separated by twenty-one years, their theological and architectural history is inextricably linked.

There was, apparently, a meetinghouse at the Hartford settlement when Hooker and his congregation arrived, but between 1638 and 1641 the community built a new one. The old one was given to Hooker, who probably used it as a barn. The new meetinghouse was one of

135 First Church: looking across the burial ground, away from the meetinghouse.

140   136 First Church: the stained-glass window depicting Thomas Hooker.

DIVINE LAW   THOMAS HOOKER   CIVIC LAW

1586   1647

THE·FOVNDATION·OF·AVTHORITY·IS·LAID·FIRSTLY·IN·THE·FREE·CONSENT·OF·THE·PEOPLE

PASTOR·OF·THIS·CHVRCH·1633—1647
TRANSPLANTED·IT·TO·HARTFORD·1636
LEADER·AMONG·THE·FOVNDERS·OF
THIS·CITY·AND·COMMONWEALTH

138 Second Church: detail of the portico.

the pyramidal roofed structures typical of the period. During the congregation's residence in this building the parish split, the result of the withdrawal of some members of the First Church in 1670. The departing company formed the South Society or Second Church, and built their own meetinghouse. After nearly one hundred years of use, the First Church voted to replace its old building. It was torn down and services were held in the State House while the new one was constructed in 1738 to 1739. The new building was an oblong side-entry clapboarded meetinghouse with a steeple. Its exterior was apparently similar to the one at Farmington, built in 1771.

There had been plans to build the 1739 meetinghouse of brick, but it was not until the First Church congregation raised its 1806 building that this idea was realized. Pews were sold and let, the size of the church's lot was increased, and construction began in March 1806. Later, more pews were sold to complete the financing. (Skilled workmen were paid about $1.33 per day, though alcohol was provided to spur their labors.) The meetinghouse was ready for dedication in December 1807.

The interiors of both Hartford meetinghouses have been radically altered over the years. Timothy Dwight described the original high pulpit at First Church, which stood opposite the front entry on the long axis of the building, according to the church, rather than the meetinghouse, plan:

137 Second Church: detail of the 1853 ceiling.

The pulpit is of varnished wood, resembling light colored mahogany, standing on fluted columns. The ascent to it is by a circular flight of stairs on each side.

This pulpit has long since disappeared. It was lowered in 1816, again in 1835, and replaced in 1851 when the pulpit wall was extended to house a platform and a new pulpit. The galleries were also lowered in 1835. Since 1851 the exterior has undergone successive redecorations and the installation of stained-glass windows on the lower level, including one depicting Hooker. The box pews were replaced with the present slips in 1851. An intriguing element of the interior is that it lacks the traditional vestibule common to most buildings constructed on the church plan. Instead, there are three separate chambers, the outer two providing stairway access to the gallery.

Both these Hartford meetinghouses are particularly notable for their exteriors. As with Center Church and United Church in New Haven, the European roots of the Hartford churches are clear. The façade of the First Church meetinghouse has a pedimented portico over its central entry, which rises on wooden Ionic columns with shadow pilasters. Panelled parapets topped by urns rise to the base of the tower. The steeple above is in four stages, the bottom one being square, and the top three octagonal. All three main stages are decorated with support columns, dentiled cornices, and balustrades topped by urns. The spire is actually a small fourth stage with a very small spire, giving the steeple a squat appearance about which Dwight commented:

> The appearance of the whole is incomplete, from not being finished with a lofty spire, but terminating in a low octagon, like the upright part of a drum light, crowned with urns surrounding the shaft, balls, and rod, common to most churches. The whole height to the vane is one hundred and sixty-five feet.

This steeple, which is constructed of wood, was probably raised by pulling the successive stages up from within the tower, in much the same fashion as at the First Baptist Church in Providence.

The equally imposing steeple of Hartford's Second Church, or South Church, is within easy view of the First Church's or Center Church, meetinghouse. Soon after the division of the parish in 1670, the Second Church must have built a meetinghouse, though dates and descriptions concerning it are sketchy. It was probably complete by 1672 and resembled the second building in which the First Church was housed. The Second Church constructed a new meetinghouse in the early 1750s, which was a simpler version of the First Church's 1739 building. When the Second Church, once again, followed in the footsteps of the First by constructing a new meetinghouse in 1826 they did not settle for a simpler structure, but built on an equally grand scale. Construction was voted in 1825, probably begun in 1826, and the meetinghouse was dedicated in 1827.

The relationship between the two brick buildings is dramatically seen in the exteriors. In most respects, the façade of the Second Church's meetinghouse is as elaborate as that of the 1806 First Church. Though the entry doors are simpler and the panels on the façade are lacking, the portico rises on Corinthian columns with matching brick shadow and corner pilasters. All three entries are under the portico. Once again, there are urn-topped parapets leading to the base of the tower. The steeple rises in four stages and it differs from the steeple of First Church in that all the stages are octagonal. The two main stages (the first and third) rise on columns while the second is a band decorated by round windows. The fourth stage is a small octagonal one. As at First Church there are urn-topped balusters; there is also no traditional spire, though the appearance is less jarring here because the steeple is thinner and more delicate in appearance. It is interesting that there is only one single tall rank of side windows instead of the usual two.

The major alteration to the interior occurred in 1853 when Minard Lafever redesigned it and installed the domed ceiling. The original pews were probably replaced at this time. In 1873, the circular window behind the pulpit was closed, a new pulpit and platform were installed and the windows were replaced. A fire did a good deal of damage in 1884, but the interior was swiftly restored.

The designs for the two meetinghouses are attributed to local builders. Daniel Wadsworth, a member of the First Church congregation, is credited with that of the First Church, while General William Hayden and Nathaniel Woodhouse, local Hartford contractors, are credited with at least building the Second Church. Certainly European pattern-books played a part in the designs and, as with their brick counterparts on the New Haven green, James Gibbs was probably the dominant influence. Hooker did not live to see the division which led to these two fine descendants of his first meetinghouse. One wonders what he would think of two such elaborate houses, built on the church plan, and along European lines, carrying on his New England Puritan/Congregationalist tradition.

140 A 19th-century photograph of Hartford, showing both its fine surviving steeples (first and third from the right).

FIRST CHURCH

Templeton, Massachusetts 1811

By 1810, the old Templeton meetinghouse had been standing for more than fifty years. It was just southeast of where the present meetinghouse stands on the town green. Moved when the new meetinghouse was built, it served as the public townhouse for the next thirty years. The new building rose to great heights, boasting a steeple unlike anything seen in the area before. The architect chosen by the Templeton congregation was Elias Carter, then of Brimfield, Massachusetts, and the builder was Jonathan Cutting, apparently a Templeton housewright.

Carter was born in Ward, Massachusetts, in 1781. His father and uncle were partners in a building business near Worcester, but Timothy, the father, was killed in a fall when Elias was only three. The interest in building was apparently passed on. Elias Carter was a wanderer. His wife later recalled that she could remember living in at least forty different places. Elias's travels apparently took him throughout the Northeast and there is evidence that he went to the South in the early nineteenth century. He must have seen many examples of architectural influences in his travels. We also know that he owned at least one of Batty Langley's English design compilations which had been passed on to him by his father.

Carter built a church in Brimfield in 1805, but it no longer stands. The earliest standing church which we can definitely ascribe to him is in Templeton, north of Brimfield near the New Hampshire border. Given the itinerant nature of his early career we can assume that he settled in Templeton for a time and there is evidence that he designed at least one house of importance there. Carter's later career is easier to trace. He built churches in Thompson (1815) and Killingly (1818), Connecticut, and the church at Mendon, Massachusetts (1820), was built from his plans. After 1828 Carter settled back in his home town, Worcester, where his work was both fine and prolific.

The Templeton meetinghouse is handsome. Though there is no porch of the Bulfinch or Benjamin style, there is a tall, shallow, pedimented portico. The corners of the façade are each decorated with two pilasters. The frieze is plain, but the cornices throughout are distinctively ornamented. The tower frieze is decorated. The entry doors are simple, with a common lintel, and above the entry are three medallions with swags and a palladian window. The most notable part of Carter's design is the steeple. The first stage is a square open-arched belfry topped by two octagonal stages and a spire. The top stage has vertically elliptical windows which match the one in the center of the portico pediment. During his

141 The façade of Elias Carter's meetinghouse. The steeple and pediment window are typical of the "run" inspired by this building.

wanderings Carter was exposed to the rural development of the church plan in meetinghouse architecture, and must have been influenced by Asher Benjamin's suggested designs. In his choice of portico rather than porch, however, and in the detailed, Wren-like steeple, Carter's work represented something of a departure. Evidence of the portico design can be found in the design of his buildings in Brimfield. The inspiration for the steeple must have come from a design-book, possibly James Gibbs's.

As intriguing as where Carter's meetinghouse design came from is the influence it had on other buildings. In our discussion of the Church on the Hill, Lenox, we observed how designs were passed from town to town. In his excellent article on the distribution of meetinghouse styles in New England, Peter Benes illustrates a number of examples, which include the Lenox group, started by Bulfinch's meetinghouse in Pittsfield. Carter's

142 The back of the meetinghouse from the cemetery: note the closed-in window frames, particularly of the palladian pulpit window in the center.

143 A view from the platform, showing the curved slip pews and Victorian casing of the gallery rail with false balusters.

144 The gallery supports: note the Victorian additions to the casings and the 19th-century pendants.

Templeton church represents the beginning of a similar stylistic "run" with successive towns copying not the Templeton church, but rather a copy of a copy. Benes has reconstructed the progress of the design as much as town records will allow.

In 1812, Troy, New Hampshire, sent two representatives to Templeton to examine Carter's meetinghouse in anticipation of building their own. The Fitzwilliam, New Hampshire, meetinghouse, very near Troy, is a striking copy of Carter's building. In Dublin, just north of the other two New Hampshire towns, the town fathers actually hired Jonathan Cutting, the master builder of the Templeton meetinghouse, as well as at least one other builder who had been involved in the Fitzwilliam building. The town of Hancock then imitated Dublin in 1819 and the run continued north through New Hampshire to Acworth (1821) and Newport (1822). Carter's distinctive steeple style was certainly popular in the vicinity. In 1823, the town of Jaffrey, near Fitzwilliam, Troy and Dublin, added a staged steeple like Templeton's to their 1775 meetinghouse, which in most other respects is similar to Farmington, Connecticut's 1771 building.

The fact that the later buildings' relationship to Templeton was generational rather than direct goes a long way toward explaining certain differences which appear along the route. While the Fitzwilliam meetinghouse is almost an exact duplicate of Templeton, by the time the design reached Hancock, the portico has turned into a porch, and in Newport the body of

145 The closing of the pulpit wall (see pl. 142) allowed this dramatically frescoed treatment of the interior in imitation of a chancel.

146 The five-headed gravestone of the Howe family.

the building is brick. Clearly, local master builders were arriving at their own architectural conclusions. The elements of Carter's form that remain relatively constant are the three stages of the steeple and the matching window in the portico or porch pediment.

The interior at Templeton was greatly changed in 1859. The box pews were replaced with long, curved ones. The high pulpit was also replaced by a platform and the pulpit wall windows were blocked up. The gallery detailing was also changed. One can assume that the pulpit at Templeton was much like the fine one at Carter's Mendon meetinghouse, which appears to have been inspired by Asher Benjamin's design. Another nineteenth-century change was the installation of stained glass. Though this has been reversed, some apparently inaccessible remains can still be seen in the palladian window over the entry. The changes at Templeton were unfortunate, but (together with surviving photographs of nineteenth-century frescoes on the pulpit wall) they represent a remarkable example of New England's rural Victorian taste.

A walk around the back of the Templeton meetinghouse is useful for two reasons. The ground drops off sharply at the back of the town green, and from the cemetery one can see the outline of the old window frames on the pulpit wall, including one of a palladian pulpit window. The cemetery itself is quite special. There are many finely carved stones, but one near the back of the meetinghouse stands out. The death of Mrs Howe and four of her children in the span of about three weeks is memorialized on one, long, five-headed stone. The cemetery then slopes down into the trees in a series of plateaux.

OLD ROUND CHURCH

Richmond, Vermont 1812

Richmond is a typical, thriving, small Vermont community, set in a northern valley near Burlington. The town provides dramatic mountain views in all directions, and is criss-crossed by both the Winooski and Huntington rivers. Its situation, ideal for farming, must have been a powerful attraction to the earliest settlers. These hardy folk first arrived in 1775 and started a settlement which was incorporated as the town of Richmond in 1794. Though the town was initially a farming community, it enjoyed an industrial boom in the late nineteenth and early twentieth centuries, with industries which employed two hundred townspeople.

The first religious organization in Richmond was formed in 1801 by Congregationalists. Other groups quickly followed. By 1812, the community included societies of Universalists, Baptists, Christians and Methodists. During the early years of the nineteenth century there was much discussion concerning the building of a meetinghouse, but as usual the issue of its siting became highly controversial. The question was settled in 1812, when two gentlemen, Isaac Glenson and Thomas Whitcomb, donated land for the purpose.

Once the site had been settled, the money-raising and building proceeded with surprising rapidity and unity. All the various denominations combined to raise funds. The Congregationalists raised $1331.84, the Universalists $1072.44, the Baptists $214.00, the Christians $201.54 and the Methodists $60.00. (In fairness, it should be pointed out that there were only two Methodists, and a very generous pair they were). The group hired a gentleman named William Rhodes to build their meetinghouse, and we must assume that it was Rhodes who came up with the design for the remarkable sixteen-sided structure which still dominates the landscape just outside Richmond.

Architectural genealogy is often complicated. It is particularly so here, because the church appears to be unique: it has long been assumed that Rhodes must have been inspired by some other building in New England, but since no similar church structure remains no one has ventured a guess as to where. Only in recent years, through the efforts of a number of scholars, have Rhodes's roots been traced, and this seems to explain the genesis of his building. The story really has two beginnings, one in Warwick, Rhode Island, and the other in Concord, New Hampshire.

In 1802, the population of Concord, New Hampshire, had grown to the point that an addition to their traditional rectangular meetinghouse was essential. Though the designer of the 1803 addition is unknown, his design is documented. The architect expanded the meetinghouse by constructing an eight-sided addition to its south side. It was remarkable that the community rejected the usual splitting of the parish and that their committee accepted the uncommon architectural form. Though this horseshoe plan was used in New England for theaters and auditoriums it was rare in church design.

A few years later the town of Claremont, New Hampshire, forty miles west of Concord, faced a similar problem and responded by expanding their meetinghouse with a similar horseshoe addition. It is in nearby Charleston, New Hampshire, that the Rhode Island part of our story begins.

William Rhodes was born in Warwick, Rhode Island, and moved to Charleston, just south of Claremont, when he was in his early twenties. Some of his mother's family were living there. He was apparently a moderately successful carpenter, and there are records of a number of land purchases by him during his few years in Charleston. In 1806, he sold his property and bought a large farm in Richmond, but he clearly maintained ties with the Charleston-Claremont region. Though the Claremont Meetinghouse addition was completed two years after his move to Richmond we can be fairly certain that he probably saw it during, or soon after, its construction.

This able scholarly detective work gave us the major clues in the solution to an architectural mystery. The design of the Old Round Church is unique in New England, being the only survivor of these structures. It did not, however, spring full-blown from the imagination of a country joiner. Rather it had, like most buildings, a traceable—and in this case a fascinating—ancestry.

147 The pulpit.

148 The gallery: note the benches at the front.

150 Looking back towards the main entry: note the wood-grained gallery railing and the stove-pipe holders on the left.

Rhodes's building is indeed very special. The interior is unusually light and airy and its sixteen sides, though individually slightly narrower than is usually the case with the horseshoe additions, create a space which gives "the devil no corner to hide around." The pulpit has been lowered and the sounding-board removed. A few of the box pews were removed to accommodate modern, secular town meetings, but many more remain than have been removed. The gallery runs along all but three of the sides. There are three doors. The exterior is very simple and, though the shape has been accented in the past by painting the framework, is now completely white. The roof is topped by an octagonal tower and a belfry which has recently been removed and restored.

Co-operative effort among churches to raise a church is extremely rare and usually does not last as long as the building. The coalition in Richmond fell apart rapidly after construction was finished, and by 1880 the town had had to take over the church. By 1973 structural problems were so serious that major restoration was necessary. The town raised $150,000—sixty times the $2500 the original building had cost. The restored church is a testament to the same strength of community evident when the church was originally raised.

149 The main entry.

THE NEW HAVEN GREEN

CENTER CHURCH
New Haven, Connecticut 1813

UNITED CHURCH
New Haven, Connecticut 1813

Three fine church buildings face the green in New Haven, all built within three years of each other: Center Church (or First Church), United Church and Trinity Episcopal Church (1814). This section will concentrate on the first two because of their remarkable architectural interest and their related histories. Just as the First and Second Church in Hartford both descend from Hooker's original Puritan congregation there, these two New Haven churches both descend from John Davenport's first congregation at this coastal settlement.

151 United Church: a view *c.* 1900.

152 Center Church: a view *c.* 1900.

153 United Church: the gallery steps in the vestibule.

154 United Church: the gallery, showing the ceiling's sunburst pattern.

Hooker's migration to Hartford and Davenport's settlement at New Haven (originally called Quinnipiac) happened within a few years of each other, both with similar goals. Davenport and Hooker were, however, quite different personalities. Some of Hooker's complexities have been touched on already; there is little need to give Davenport the same treatment here. He was typical of the first generation of New England's Puritan orthodoxy, firm and certain in his delineation of the Way. His return to Boston in 1668, after thirty years in New Haven, followed by his immovable adherence to Puritan conservatism and his refusal to accept the Half-Way Covenant, caused the division which resulted in the founding of Boston's Third Church, later Old South. The New Haven settlement also differs from Hartford commercially. Certainly Hooker's parishioners were looking for rich land in the Connecticut River valley, but the commercial side of the New Haven enterprise was more blatantly represented. Davenport's partner in the project was Theophilus Eaton, a wealthy

155,156 Center Church: the façade, and the interior, showing the Davenport window on the pulpit wall.

London merchant. Though his Puritan credentials were sound enough, one of his main interests in the establishment of the New Haven colony was the creation of a vital trade link between Massachusetts and New Amsterdam, with New Haven as its center. Eaton's dream was never realized.

Eaton first came to Quinnipiac in late 1637, left and returned in the spring of 1638. Davenport held his first open-air service on April 18th. A little over a year later the free planters of the settlement gathered in a barn to address both civil and theological issues. Their establishment of a General Court shows their independent nature, which remained evident even after its absorption by Connecticut in 1664. In November 1639, the Court determined to build the community's first meetinghouse.

This first building was a square, pyramidal, or hip-roofed building, much like many of the earliest houses. From the start, it had structural problems. In 1669, all efforts at saving the building apparently having been exhausted, a new one, of similar design, was raised. This building served until the middle of the eighteenth century. The drummer, who stood in the turret to summon worshippers, was replaced by a bell in 1681. New Haven grew rapidly, and there was too little space in the second meetinghouse within a few years of its construction. By the late 1690s every available square inch was taken up by seating of one sort or another. Boys were allotted space on the gallery steps. An addition was built, but in 1727 the continuing crush led to the construction of a third gallery.

The cramp was undoubtedly alleviated by the separation of some of the membership in 1740. We will discuss this schism in greater detail below as United Church was a direct descendant. Regardless of the division, by the 1750s the parishioners of the First Church were ready to build again. The new brick meetinghouse was usable in 1757, though it was probably not completed until 1764. The surviving pictures of it indicate that it was similar to Old South in Boston, with round-headed windows, a side entry with the pulpit opposite, and an open-arched belfry and spire.

In 1812 the congregation decided to build a new brick meetinghouse. No clear reason for the decision has surfaced: the most likely explanation is that the parishioners felt that their building was old-fashioned. It is certainly true that there had been a revolution in design since the raising of their "Old Brick" house a little more than fifty years earlier. All the earlier buildings had been built on the meetinghouse plan, and, literally, on the town green. The new building was designed on the church plan, and faced the green. This necessitated the covering of part of the old burial ground: the problem was solved by the creation of a crypt, a rarity in New England.

The complicated relationship of architects and master builders is a subject of contention in the histories of both these New Haven Congregational churches. In the case of First Church, or Center Church as it is now known because of its position on the green, one can trace most of the information. Apparently on the strength of his meetinghouse in Northampton, which representatives of the New Haven building committee traveled to see, the first builder was Isaac Damon. Damon and his assistant were commissioned to build the meetinghouse from plans purchased directly from Asher Benjamin in Boston for $40. By the end of the project, however, Damon's name had disappeared from the church records. Whether Damon was present when construction began in 1813 is uncertain, but probable. By the time the building was suitable for use (reportedly in late 1814, though it might have been somewhat later), there is no question that Damon's associate, Ithiel Town[e], a bridge builder like Damon, was in charge.

Regardless of who did what when, the result at Center Church is superb. Indeed, it is sometimes considered to be the most beautiful of New England's ecclesiastical buildings, particularly in its exterior. It certainly towers above most of its early nineteenth-century contemporaries, both literally and figuratively. The origins of the design are clear. Though Benjamin may not have drawn as directly on James Gibbs as Joseph Brown did for his steeple at Providence, it is clear that the Boston architect was inspired by Gibbs and particularly by St Martin-in-the-Fields, London. The New Haven church is a distinct derivative. This is most evident in the balustrade which surrounds the roofline, the wide porch, and in elements of the steeple.

The impressive pedimented portico at Center Church rests on tall wooden Doric columns with shadow and corner pilasters which are repeated at the back of the building. The portico is intriguingly decorated, with an intricate carved ornament on the face of the pediment, and a frieze which includes carved bulls' skulls. The three arched entries are within the portico, with round-headed windows above. The central entry juts out, creating a porch within the portico. The design of the tower repeats the arched brickwork of the rest of the building: the tower arches have round-headed windows within them like the upper rank of the side windows, while the lower rank of side windows are only slightly arched. The distinctive roof balustrade runs along both sides and is topped by urns. The steeple rises in three stages, with a spire above: the first two are square, while the top one is octagonal. The first stage has an arched frieze to accommodate a four-faced clock, while the second has keystone arches within pedimented porches, and corner pilasters. The third stage has engaged Corinthian columns at each corner, and round-headed windows on every other panel. The top two stages have urns at each upper corner. There is an account of the raising of the steeple which indicates that it was pulled up from within the tower, stage by stage. Norman Isham uses the description to support his theory of the construction of the tower at First Baptist Church in Providence.

The interior at Center Church has been changed to some degree, the major remodeling taking place in 1842. The original slip pews were replaced, and the galleries and pulpit were lowered. Later the pulpit was replaced and the original somehow made its way to Hawaii. There was at one time a frescoed pulpit wall which imitated a chancel. The pushing out of the pulpit wall was later considered, but happily it was never accomplished. Stained-glass windows were installed, but all except the one of John Davenport on the present pulpit wall are gone. The ceiling is magnificently domed.

The separation of New Haven's Congregational parish came as a result of the Great

157 United Church: the back, showing the pediment over the later pulpit recess.

158 Center Church: the back, showing the roofline balustrade, the rear pilasters and the arched brickwork.

Awakening, the religious revival which swept New England ignited by the preaching of men such as Edwards and Whitefield. Two years after Whitefield visited New Haven, in 1740, the "New Lights"—those who approved of Whitefield and responded to the revivalist power of his preaching—withdrew from the First Church and founded their own. The separation was not formalized until 1759, when they became known as the White Haven Society. The disruptive troubles were not over, however. Ten years later a rift developed in the new parish, ironically caused by their pastor, Edwards's son Jonathan Jr. He was apparently even less pastoral than his father, and his dry preaching and personality displeased many members of the congregation. A new church was formed in 1771 and was incorporated as the Fair Haven Society in 1774. Both names for these separatist groups spring from unknown sources, though it has been suggested that White Haven was a combined form of Whitefield and New Haven.

The White Haven group was not allowed by the town to put up a meetinghouse on the green. Even when the new group found an alternate site, the opposition was fierce. When their meetinghouse was ready to be raised, and all the timber had been cut to length, some people, probably representatives of the "Old Lights" from the First Church, cut them in half during the night. The timbers had to be replaced and the new Society had to post guards until their building was raised. Not much is known of the first house, though it seems it had box

159 Trinity Church, New Haven. Ithiel Town's Gothic church stands right next to Center Church on the green.

160 United Church: the center aisle. Note the later pulpit recess and the ceiling dome above, with its decorative rim; also the sunburst decoration to the ceiling corners.

161 United Church: the façade.

pews and a gallery. After a further division in 1771 the Fair Haven Society built a meetinghouse facing the green on approximately the same site where the United Church now stands. So, at the time of the Revolution, there were three Congregational meeting-houses in New Haven: the "Old Brick" of the First Church, and the houses of both the Fair Haven and White Haven Societies. The two separatist societies were rejoined in 1810, and determined to build a new meetinghouse at the Fair Haven meetinghouse site, facing the green. Consequently, the two old rival churches found themselves building new houses at about the same time and on adjoining lots.

The question of who designed the United Church meetinghouse is even more complicated than in the case of the Center Church building. (The United Church was not called by that name until later in the nineteenth century as the result of yet another union, but in the interests of simplification it will be referred to as such from now on.) David Hoadley, a builder, has long been credited as architect for this and a number of other fine Connecticut meetinghouses of the early nineteenth century. J. Frederick Kelly, in his exhaustive study of Connecticut meetinghouses, has compelling evidence that Hoadley was both architect and master builder. He cites the hiring of Hoadley in late 1812, and the vote of thanks delivered to him on November 29th, 1815 as "Architect," after completion of the project. The congregation thanked him "for the substantial, elegant, and workmanlike manner in which he has performed his contract, and that he be recommended to the Public for his skill and fidelity in his profession." Kelly points out that this citation is separate from the one delivered to the contractors. He also questions, with justification, the attribution of the design to Ebenezer Johnson, a local contractor and shoemaker who was later a member of the church. We have probably not heard the last of this discussion. It is useful to remember that Center Church, although built from a plan by Asher Benjamin, is regularly attributed to Ithiel Town as architect rather than master builder. Despite Kelly's stand, there is still much scholarly uncertainty: the jury is still out on this complex question.

As with Center Church, once one puts aside the question of authorship, what remains is the pleasure of the building itself. It would be hard to find two such distinguished churches standing "cheek by jowl" anywhere. Though United is slightly less grand than its neighbor, it is no less elegant. There are certain basic similarities in the exterior: both buildings are brick, with indented intersticed arches housing windows and entries, and the ranks of side windows are strikingly similar. The major differences are in the façades, towers and steeples.

The porch at United Church is a more traditional New England form. There is no roofline balustrade, so the porch pediment mirrors that of the roof. The pediment rests on engaged and fluted wooden Ionic columns. The pediment and roof have dentiled cornices but the front friezes are plain. The tower has a single round window in each side. The steeple is not as tall as the one at Center Church, and is quite different, rising in two main stages with a dome rather than a spire. The first stage is a square arched belfry with an entablature above including an arch similar to the one in the first stage at Center Church. The dome stage is a round lantern decorated with engaged Ionic columns, round-headed windows and a dentiled cornice with urns above.

The interior at United Church is much like that of its neighbor, particularly in its massive domed ceiling. In 1849, the pulpit wall was pushed out, but the old pulpit was retained. The pews were redesigned at the same time. In the late nineteenth century, the rear gallery was lowered and the stairs were altered accordingly. In both these New Haven buildings, the columns which support the gallery do not run from floor to ceiling because of the breadth of the great ceiling domes.

It would be inappropriate to conclude this section on New Haven without at least a brief mention of the Episcopal church which stands on the other side of Center Church, also facing the green. By the middle of the eighteenth century, the Anglican community in New Haven had grown sufficiently to justify building a church. The first building resembled the Anglican church at Stratford, Connecticut, with a tower and spire and the main entry through the tower. In the early nineteenth century, the Episcopal church grew, both in Connecticut and in New Haven. In 1812, the Trinity parish petitioned the town for the right to build on the green, and the town assented. Building probably commenced in the spring of 1814, but the massive stone building was not consecrated until 1816. Town, managing to keep himself very busy in New Haven, was the architect/builder. He described the building thus:

> The Gothic style of architecture has been chosen and adhered to in the erection of this Church, as being . . . better suited to the solemn purposes of religious worship. It . . . is in line with two Ecclesiastical Churches, lately erected in the same street and square; and perhaps the situation of these three Churches, in a line nearly equidistant, and viewed in connection with the other buildings round the public square, is not surpassed by any arrangement of the kind in this country. This Church is 103 feet long, and 74 feet wide, exclusive of the tower at the front end, which is 25 feet square, and projects forward half its size . . . the walls are raised 38 feet, with a hard granite . . . and layed with their natural faces out, and so selected and fitted as to form small but irregular joints, which are pointed. These natural faces present various shades of brown and iron-rust; and when damp, especially, the different shades appear very deep and rich; at the same time conveying to the mind an idea of durability and antiquity, which may be very suitably associated with this style of architecture. There are five windows on a side and two in the rear end . . . all glazed with diamond glass.

It was considered a masterpiece of Gothic architecture when built, and remains one of the remarkable early Gothic buildings in the country.

It is important to remember that, while all this building was going on in this coastal Connecticut town, the United States was in the midst of the War of 1812. Most of the timber for framing these buildings came down the Connecticut coast by ship, and had to run the British blockade. Legend has it that the first two times Commodore Hardy stopped American vessels claiming to bear nothing but timber for church building he let them pass, stating that "he made no war on religion." The third time he once again let them pass, this time exclaiming: "Don't these damned Yankees do anything but build churches?"

FIRST CHURCH OF CHRIST

Lancaster, Massachusetts 1816

163 A view of the meetinghouse showing the massive arches which Thomas Hearsey adapted from Bulfinch's design.

162 The pulpit, a fine example of Bulfinch-Benjamin design.

harles Bulfinch was America's first great professional architect. He almost single-handedly changed the face of Boston, and his completion of the Capitol and his residence in Washington did much to shape that city's architectural heritage—though there are many buildings there for which he must not be blamed. By 1815, his career was in full flower. He had already built the Massachusetts State House (1795), University Hall at Harvard (1813), and numerous houses and some churches in Boston. On the basis of his reputation alone he might have been sought by the Unitarians of Lancaster. But Bulfinch, product of a good Boston family, was also a Unitarian and a devoted friend to William Ellery Channing, the religious architect of nineteenth-century Unitarianism.

The Lancaster parish, once Congregational, now Unitarian, has a long history. The town's charter was granted in 1653, and the first meetinghouse was built about 1657. The second meetinghouse, built in 1684, was destroyed in an Indian attack in 1704, the same year as the famous Deerfield massacre. The present Bulfinch church is the fifth Lancaster house of worship. Its pastor at the time of construction was Nathaniel Thayer. Dr Thayer was also a friend of Channing, as well as William Emerson, John Kirkland and others who spearheaded the Unitarian movement.

The problem of a site for the new church was solved surprisingly easily. Captain Benjamin Lee agreed to sell two acres of his farm for $633.33. These acres now comprise the Lancaster town green. These typical New Englanders, always available for a good democratic town tussle, still managed to find something to argue about. Bulfinch's design called for only one entrance rather than the several which the people were accustomed to. This controversial notion led to a fierce struggle about the positioning of the building. The discussion came down to a choice between a western or a southern entrance. In his *History of the Town of Lancaster* (1879) the Rev. Abijah Marvin related the following tale about the episode. After there had been a good deal of discussion about who would be inconvenienced by which placement, a gentleman named John Willard rose and suggested that the new edifice be built on a contraption similar to a "lazy-susan" so that "each man, as he came up, could take hold of the handle and bring the house round towards himself." A brilliant solution, if impractical. The Rev. Marvin, in typical Victorian fashion, felt Willard must have been eccentric; nevertheless Willard's motion—whether or not the humor was intentional—reduced the discussion to its appropriate level. Later, committees were formed and a southerly entrance was approved.

The cornerstone was laid on July 9th, 1816, with much pomp, and the big brick church was raised in just 157 days. This was quite an accomplishment under any circumstances, made even more remarkable given the cold summer of 1816—it snowed on the Fourth of July. Much of the credit for this building must go to master builder Thomas Hearsey (Hersey), not only for its efficient construction but also for crucial elements of its design. This church offers ample evidence of the importance of the on-site master builder. Hearsey, aged fifty-three when he undertook the project, was no newcomer to construction. He came from a family of builders in Hingham and had worked in Boston as a housewright for a number

164 The center aisle.

of years. It has even been suggested that he may have done some work for Bulfinch. By the time he accepted the Lancaster job he had moved to nearby Harvard, Massachusetts. This move, together with the liberties he took with the Bulfinch design, indicate that he was probably a fairly independent character. An often-quoted 1826 description of the finished building will still serve, as few changes have been made to the building. The author is Joseph Willard, writing in his *Topographical and Historical Sketches of the Town of Lancaster* (1826):

> The body of the building is 74 by 66 feet, with a porch, portico, tower and cupola. The portico is 48 by 17 feet, of square brick columns, arched with pilasters, entablature, and pediment of the Doric order; the vestibule, or porch, is 48 by 19 feet and contains the gallery stairs; the tower is 21 feet square; the cupola is circular, and of singular beauty;—it is surrounded with a colonade of 12 fluted pillars, with entablature, and cornice, of the Ionic order; above which is an Attic encircled with a festoon drapery, the whole surmounted by a dome, balls and vane. The height from the ground is about 120 feet. Inside, the front of the

gallery is of ballustrade work, and is supported by ten fluted pillars of the Doric order, and has a clock in front, presented by a gentleman of the society. The pulpit rests on eight fluted columns, and four pilasters of the Ionic order: the upper section is supported by six Corinthian columns also fluted, and is lighted by a circular headed window, ornamented with double pilasters fluted; entablature and cornice of the Corinthian order; this is decorated with a curtain and drapery from a Parisian model, which, with the materials, were presented by a friend; they are of rich green figured satin. A handsome Pulpit Bible was presented also by a friend, and a bell weighing 1300 lbs was given by gentlemen of the town.

165 The tower: note the swags, Ionic columns on the belfry and the volutes—another Hearsey addition.

166 The carriage sheds next to the meetinghouse are among New England's finest surviving examples.

Hearsey's major change was to the portico. Judging by a later drawing based on Bulfinch's original, we can be quite sure that Bulfinch planned to make the two side arches of the portico smaller, with swags above. This would have reflected the relative sizes of the entry doors within the portico. Apparently, Hearsey also added the volutes on the tower, though Harold Kirker points out that they are consistent with those on Bulfinch's Holy Cross Church in Boston (1801).

The interior is little changed. In 1869 and 1900 the interior detailing was augmented, but the basic form, including the mahogany box pews, the gallery and the magnificent pulpit, have not been altered. Stoves and piping were added in 1827 and the main body of the church is still heated in this fashion. During the last third of the nineteenth century an attempt was made to divide the building into two floors, but the long-term objections of the then minister, George Bartol, forced the abandonment of the idea. The compromise was to add the present parish house. The surviving carriage sheds at Lancaster are some of New England's best.

Why Hearsey decided to build the arched portico in the way he did, is, for the moment, unknown. His decision, however, is certainly what gives the church such a strikingly modern look. There can be no question about the result of the Bulfinch-Hearsey alchemy. The exterior was not painted originally, as so many contemporary brick buildings were. It was painted a dull brown in 1869; in this unfortunate incarnation it was known in Lancaster as the "drab church." Though the inhabitants are still somewhat shamefaced about the episode they should be proud of their early decision, in 1900, to strip the paint and to return the church to its past glory.

CONGREGATIONAL CHURCH

Warren, Connecticut 1818

167 The steeple at Warren.

The placing of New England meetinghouses on the town greens is mentioned in the very beginning of this book. Warren's green is not a green at all, at least not in the most traditional sense. It is really a junction of two small country roads, with a few houses, the town offices, and general store and the old cemetery scattered along the arms of the crossroads. Though there is a traffic light, the roads are lightly traveled. The view from the hilltop is sensational. But what transforms this quiet rural crossroads into a breathtaking scene is a meetinghouse which stands near the height of land. Nowhere in New England is there a meetinghouse more beautifully sited.

The town is named after Dr Joseph Warren, the legendary Patriot hero killed at the Battle of Bunker Hill. He was also the man who sent Paul Revere and William Dawes to warn the Minutemen of Lexington and Concord on the night of April 18th, 1775. Warren was officially memorialized in this Connecticut town when it was incorporated in 1786, but the area had actually been settled earlier, and was originally part of the town of Kent. The church

168 The meetinghouse on the hill at Warren.

was first organized in 1750, listing itself at that time as the Society of East Greenwich in Kent. As was often the case, the early history of this New England parish was dominated by one preacher of exceptional tenure and presence. Though Sylvanus Osborn, an early settler, shepherded the Warren church in its formative years, it was Peter Starr, installed in 1771, who built this parish. Starr's pastorate spanned fifty-seven critical years in the history of both Warren and the nation. He succeeded in giving the young parish a permanent place in the community and established a fund to support the Warren ministry. In the twilight of his career Starr saw to the building of the present meetinghouse.

The meetinghouse Starr inherited from Osborn was little more than four years old. According to Agnes Strong, it "had a startling resemblance to a respectable barn." It had no steeple, and was never painted, either outside or in. There were three entries, with the pulpit and main southern entry on the short axis, according to the meetinghouse plan. There was a gallery and box pews. Seating was apparently a topic for heated debate, and there are a number of records of new committees to resolve disputes on the issue. In 1800 some repairs were made, but by 1814 the old building was so dilapidated that the townspeople called it the "Lord's barn." In the spring of 1814 a committee was formed to decide whether to repair the old house, and having decided not to, they were charged to "circulate subscriptions and get Money to build a Meeting House." In 1815, it was determined that the money would be paid back by selling the completed pews and that the new meetinghouse should be "on the Green near where the oald [sic] one now stands." This decision was modified the next year to "in part where the old one now stands." Money was a problem, and loans had to be obtained. By 1818, the congregation was determined to go ahead, and the old meetinghouse came down. Its remains were used in the new building and "also for sheds on the green." The committee apparently hired James Jennings of Weston to build their meetinghouse. Jennings later built the fine brick meetinghouse at Sharon, Connecticut, which is similar in form; we know that Jennings's Warren design was also used, at least in part, for the building at Derby, Connecticut, in 1820. The Warren building is in fact a small rural version of a series of Connecticut meetinghouses built in the first quarter of the nineteenth century. The type appears as early as 1813 in Norfolk, and as late as 1829 in Guilford and Litchfield. As with the buildings inspired by Elias Carter's Templeton house, there are variations, particularly in the use of porticos and porches. The steeples are the most constant feature, all rising from the tower in two octagonal stages, topped by a spire.

Though the people of Warren may have been strapped for cash, they managed to build a meetinghouse comparable to its better-heeled cousins. Although smaller than most, it is exquisite in its design and detail. The steeple suffered an unfortunate restoration after it was struck by lightning in 1891. In recent years, however, it has been returned to its previous form, which is much in keeping with the style mentioned above. The tower rises above a simple pedimented and pilastered porch, with three pilastered doorways topped by keystone architrave fanlights. There are double-hung windows above the entry doors, another mark of this type of meetinghouse. There are no windows in the façade other than those in the porch, a design different from that of the others of this style. Though this overall form may seem

169 The restored pulpit and palladian window.

170 A view of the meetinghouse *c.* 1910.

simple at first glance, there is careful detail here as well. The porch pediment window is a rare form, and the delicate detail on the friezes below the dentiled cornices on the pediments and tower are fine.

The interior of the Warren meetinghouse exhibits the same simplicity of design combined with attention to detail. The central ceiling is barrel-vaulted, while the gallery ceilings are flat. The rear gallery used to be curved, but in 1877 was brought out in a straight line to accommodate the choir. The fluted columns run from floor to ceiling, and the Ionic capitals are fine, as are the delicate swag details on the gallery railing. This kind of attention was also lavished on the grained butternut pulpit. Though the original pulpit was removed in 1859 and replaced with a platform, enough was saved and rediscovered to recreate it in the mid-1950s. Pieces of it were retrieved from a number of nearby attics, including the fine pillars it rests on. The carving was done by Peter Starr's grandnephew, Frederick.

> He has done the work of finishing off the interior of the church, including the High Pulpit & all the molding and was greatly interested in the fine appearance of the building.

This wording implies that he might have worked the exterior details as well. At the same time as the pulpit was removed, the present slip pews were installed, and the floor of the interior was raised so that it is slightly more than two feet higher than the porch vestibule. Concurrent with the restoration of the pulpit, the palladian pulpit window was also reinstated. Stoves were installed in 1833 after a notably protracted war between the "stove party" and

171 The interior from the gallery: note the floor to ceiling columns and their finely carved capitals.

the "anti-stove party." A furnace was installed in the basement in 1906.

Despite the raised floor and the later pews, this lovely church at Warren is much as it was when the Rev. Mr Starr mounted the pulpit stairs to deliver his fiftieth anniversary sermon in 1822, at the age of seventy-eight:

> I have lived to bury all my first church, and most of my congregation . . . [in future] you may safely hope and calculate to obtain a better minister than your old one, but you must not expect to obtain so cheap a one. Be not so anxious to obtain a cheap one as a good one . . . lest, while you starve your minister, you starve your own souls and the souls of your children.

A good point, no doubt. Notwithstanding the feeding of "your minister," however, the meetinghouse which Starr saw replace the old "Lord's barn" is still a feast for the eye, and still serves the descendants of his congregation.

176

CONGREGATIONAL CHURCH

Avon, Connecticut 1818

We have already traced the history of the Farmington, Connecticut, meetinghouse back to Hooker's settlement in Hartford. The church at Avon also has roots in that settlement, as Avon was originally an outgrowth of Farmington called Northington. Farmington was a successful settlement which, for some years, dwarfed Hartford in size and productivity. As was so often the case, success begat expansion and expansion in turn brought forth a desire for independent churches and towns. By the middle of the eighteenth century, when Farmington was already a hundred years old, the families to the north sought an independent

172 The curve of the rear gallery railing with the ceiling above.

parish. The trip to Farmington for the meeting was arduous, particularly in the winter months. Probably reluctant to give up their jurisdiction, Farmington invoked a fairly common compromise called "Winter Privileges." This allowed the families in the northern part of the parish to worship in their homes during snowbound months. But the numbers north of Farmington continued to grow, and after some struggle they were given permission to form the Second Church of Farmington, or Northington Parish, in 1751.

Within three years the new church had built a meetinghouse, a typical barn-like clapboarded structure with galleries and more than one entrance. This meetinghouse served for almost sixty years but then became delapidated. As at Warren, it came to be known as the "Lord's Barn" and by the early 1800s the parish was prepared to replace it. The Northington community was a busy one: the turnpike from Albany to Hartford passed through it and the town had grown, thanks to milling and farming. There were two main population centers, one to the northeast and the other to the west. The inevitable squabble about the siting of the new house was exacerbated by the fact that the Farmington River passed between the two centers. The argument, which lasted about a decade, finally reached a crisis when the old building burned down in 1817 in rather suspicious circumstances. The only possible solution was to split the Northington parish, but even this was not easy. The vote following the fire stood at 44 to 39 in favor of building in the western community, which eventually came to be known as West Avon.

David Hoadley, whose actual role in the construction of the United Church in New Haven is a somewhat controversial issue, reappears in Avon. Kelly once again supports the theory that Hoadley was the architect and master builder, and produces intriguing documentation as a result of careful detective work. He points to a contract between the

173 A photograph of Avon, *c.*1890, with the meetinghouse on the far left.

174 An early photograph of the meetinghouse, showing the first Avon parish house: note the shutters.

175 The meetinghouse.

building committee and Hoadley to do the "joiner work." Kelly suggests that the foundations of the building were probably already laid at this time; however, there is no evidence of a plan. The contract was specifically for "framing and raising" a meetinghouse "agreeable to a plan of sd house now before us." There is no reference to the plan being Hoadley's. Kelly also points to the statement of payment of $2150 to Hoadley for "building and finishing" a meetinghouse. Despite conclusive evidence of Hoadley's participation, there is nothing to prove him the architect. The theory that Hoadley was a skilled master builder rather than a seminal designer persists. The Avon church, like the one at Warren, falls into a group of churches of similar style built in the early nineteenth century. Hoadley was certainly connected with the construction of some of them, possibly including the early one at Norfolk (1813), but there does not appear to be sufficient information to claim, as has been done, that he in some way authored the type.

The Avon house is an excellent example of the style in question and bears some striking similarities to the Warren building. It is somewhat grander, though not necessarily finer. The pedimented porch has Ionic pilasters and three arched entries with windows above. The entries have simple pilasters and keystone architraves around the fanlights. The central entry is slightly wider than the others. The pediment has a plain face with dentiled cornices, mirroring the roof pediment. The tower is simple with a circular medallion in the hemisphere pattern on the front face. The steeple has two octagonal stages, the first of which is decorated with Ionic columns and louvered keystone arches while the second has decorated panels. The spire is octagonal and shingled, giving it a ribbed appearance. The tower and the lower two stages are topped by balustrades with urns above. The upper two of these are of Chippendale type design as are the ones at the later Cheshire meetinghouse. One difference between the façade at Avon and the one at Warren is that Avon has a set of double-hung windows in the body of the church at each side of the porch.

The most apparent change to the interior of the Avon meetinghouse was the closing of the pulpit wall windows when the first parish house was added at the back of the building in 1857. The pulpit has been replaced by a platform. The present pews date from 1854. There was a serious fire in 1876 which necessitated extensive repairs, and frescoes were added at that time. There are two tiers of Ionic columns, the first supporting the finely carved gallery-rails and the second rising to the ceiling, the center of which is raised. The entablatures and cornices are all dentiled. The most graceful feature of the interior is the retention of the curved rear wall whose shape is mirrored by the gallery. At Warren the gallery-rail is brought out in a straight line, which is far less attractive. On the other hand, the closing of the pulpit wall windows at Avon is a disappointment when compared to the restored pulpit wall at Warren.

These two meetinghouses were built about fifty miles apart. They present another illustration of the intriguing pattern of stylistic dissemination in New England. Why were these two buildings so similar in overall form? Once again, one meetinghouse has influenced a group of others. The Norfolk, Connecticut, meetinghouse is probably the common factor. We know that the Avon Building Committee demanded that their building be of equal beauty

176 A detail of the façade.

177 The center aisle at Avon showing the closed pulpit wall.

to Norfolk, which actually means that they wanted a similar building. There is every reason to believe that a similar request was made at Warren, or that James Jennings, who built the Warren meetinghouse, was familiar with the Norfolk design. The present portico on the entrance bay at the Norfolk church is a twentieth-century addition. When the meetinghouses at Avon and Warren were built, the stylish Norfolk building had a pilastered porch much like the ones that remain at the other two towns.

FIRST CHURCH

Springfield, Massachusetts 1818

In March 1819 an advertisement appeared in Springfield announcing the fate of the old meetinghouse, which had been raised in 1752. It was "To Be Sold at Public Vendue, unless sooner disposed of at private sale," and there are later records of pieces of the interior being sold at auction. The fate of the old meetinghouse in New England towns when a new one was built was various, ranging from the use of the old timbers in other structures, sometimes including the new meetinghouse, as at Hingham, to just leaving the old building standing, as at Brooklyn and Wickford. It is clear that soon after the final service in the old meetinghouse on April 25th, 1819, the building in Springfield was dismantled. The new meetinghouse, begun in 1818, was largely complete. Though it is now dwarfed by office buildings around Court Square, its spire originally towered over all its neighbors and must have been visible for miles up and down the Connecticut River.

Springfield's 1818 meetinghouse was the fourth in the town's long history. William Pynchon, who led the first band of settlers to this spot in 1636, was a founder of the Massachusetts Bay Company and a prominent member of the early Puritan community in New England. He arrived in 1630 and founded Roxbury. His fifteen years at Springfield were successful, and his community leadership largely unchallenged. When in 1639 Hartford, Windsor and Wethersfield adopted the Fundamental Orders, basically a frame of government for the Connecticut River Valley, Pynchon refused to join and instead cemented ties with the Massachusetts General Court. This situation points up an interesting duality in Springfield, largely due to its geography. While it has always been a Connecticut River town and has many ties with nearby Hartford, its political center has always been Boston. Even though it is on the eastern side of the river, Springfield is the business capital of western Massachusetts.

The first minister arrived in Springfield a year after Pynchon's band, though the first meetinghouse was not built until 1645. It had "two turrets for a bell and a watch house." Cramped quarters led to this building being replaced in 1677, and the third meetinghouse was put up in 1752. All the parish's meetinghouses have been located in the center of Springfield. The growth of both the church and the town led to the third meetinghouse being replaced, though the decision was not universally well received, for both sentimental and theological reasons. The parish leadership's determination to forge ahead with the plan may have exacerbated the divisions, which led to the departure of the liberal or Unitarian segment of the church's congregation in early 1819 while the First Church's new meetinghouse was still under construction.

178 The present interior, showing the fine domed ceiling.

179 The interior at Springfield in 1881.

The architect for this divisive structure was not from Springfield. Simon Sanborn, the local master builder, was not called on to build this meetinghouse, although, ironically, he did build the first meetinghouse for the departed brethren. Instead, Dr Osgood and his congregation at the First Church awarded the contract to Captain Isaac Damon. Damon, apparently the quintessential nineteenth-century builder/architect, was particularly well known for his bridges. He was responsible for most of the spans which crossed the Connecticut during his era, and for others as far afield as the Penobscot, Mohawk, Hudson and Ohio Rivers. The Springfield congregation probably hired Damon on the strength of his work in 1812 on the meetinghouse just a few miles north in Northampton. The Northampton church, now gone, was a massive and elaborate building which Damon built probably from designs of Asher Benjamin, and was reminiscent of Benjamin's Old West Church in Boston (1806). If the Springfielders were hoping for a similar building they must have been sorely disappointed. Damon's Springfield church is a far simpler, more graceful building, on classic lines.

It is of typical oblong form with two ranks of windows. The pedimented portico is

180 Court Square in 1874.

supported by six hand-hewn Doric columns, with shadow and corner pilasters and a fine detailed front cornice and frieze. The frieze is strikingly similar to that at Center Church, New Haven. This is not surprising considering Ithiel Town's and Captain Damon's associations with each other and their probable—if short-lived—association with the New Haven church. Damon's clearest signature, however, is in the tower, and this is his most graceful in this style. It rises in three main stages. The lower two are square with arches and pilasters on the panels. The uppermost stage is circular, with pilasters topped by a small spire. The weathercock was brought from England for the 1752 meetinghouse. The depth of the portico and the slightly exaggerated projection of the tower and its size gives this church a more substantial feel than many of its contemporaries in the area.

The original interior was extensively altered in 1864, though the basic form of Damon's giant domed ceiling and galleries remains. The high pulpit is long gone, replaced by a platform, which is backed by a screen with the organ and choir behind. This configuration has been in place since 1881. Before that the congregation used to turn and face the organ to sing hymns. A contiguous parish house was added in 1874. The old pews were replaced, the gallery was lowered and the walls were frescoed in high Victorian style. A chandelier, now gone, was hung from the center of the dome. In 1924, it was decided to restore the building to its early nineteenth-century lines; not a complete restoration, but a general return to its less garish roots.

Damon's fine church was dedicated on August 19th, 1819, exactly one year after the cornerstone was laid. The pews did not sell terrifically—the recent division in the congregation might have been responsible for this. Damon supported the project by purchasing four pews for a total of $785 dollars, probably with the intention of reselling them. The church has hosted some remarkable gatherings including the lying-in-state of John Quincy Adams, a concert by the singer Jenny Lind and an oration by the Hungarian patriot Louis Kossuth. The design has endured and despite the diminished stature of the church it still dominates the square. An account at the time of the church's dedication hoped "that he who walks around our holy dwelling may ever be justified in making a good report." So far Captain Damon's graceful church is doing just fine.

181 The square today.

182 The interior viewed from the platform.

SOUTH
CONGREGATIONAL CHURCH

Newport, New Hampshire 1822

Newport's first settlers came from Connecticut in the 1760s. Legend has it that the first six or seven men, led by one Stephen Wilcox, arrived on the Sabbath and worshipped under a spreading tree. This kind of story is often repeated in New England lore. There were certainly regular meetings for worship with deacons officiating prior to the formal incorporation of Newport's church in 1779. The people gathered in private homes, meeting for some time in the log cabin of a man named Robert Lane. Following the construction of a "Proprietor's House" in 1773, they probably gathered there. The increase of population during the 1770s led to the formation of the church, but it was not until 1793 that their first meetinghouse was erected.

183 The first meetinghouse which served the community from 1793 until 1823.

184 The gallery, with its mid-19th-century pews.

A woodcut of this building survives. It was a typical oblong meetinghouse, with the entry on the side, a porch at one end, and a tower at the other. In most respects other than the tower this building seems to have been similar to the one at Rockingham, Vermont, though it was somewhat simpler. The woodcut indicates that it was shingled in much the same fashion as the meetinghouse at Waldoboro, Maine. There were carriage sheds on the site. The exterior was apparently painted yellow, while the interior was unpainted. There was a gallery, high pulpit, sounding-board and box pews which probably had spindled rails. The raising of this first meetinghouse on June 26th, 1793, was probably accompanied by the usual revelry. Whether or not the ensuing tragedy was related to rum we will never know but, sober or not, a young man, son of the pastor of the Baptist church in New London, New Hampshire, fell to his death. Despite this unfortunate incident, the meetinghouse served until the present one was built. The old building was sold to one Jonas Cutting who apparently moved it and transformed it into a barn.

This first meetinghouse was built on the west side of the Sugar River which runs near Newport on to Claremont, and eventually into the Connecticut River. In 1884, a turnpike was built, running past Newport and on to the north. Though the road served Newport, it was too much trouble to route it across the river twice in order to provide access to the

186 The façade of the meetinghouse in the fall. Note the fine "Templeton-type" steeple.

center of town. When the turnpike stayed east of the river the gradual movement of the town became inevitable. In 1818 the Newport congregation installed a new pastor, James Wheelock, son of Eleazar Wheelock, who had established Dartmouth College at Hanover, northwest of Newport. "He was a man of scholarly taste, ardent and energetic," and his installation precipitated a religious revival resulting in one hundred new church members in 1819 alone. A merchant named James Breck had arrived in Newport a few years before Wheelock and established a successful business. He built his home and offices near the turnpike, east of the river and south of the old town center. The highway, the revival and the commercial success were probably the three most critical factors in the siting of the present church. The old building was on the wrong side of the river, the revival probably made it cramped in any case, and the money was moving east, albeit not very far east.

We have discussed the stylistic descendants of Elias Carter's church at Templeton,

185 A side view showing the fine arched brickwork.

Massachusetts. The "run" of related buildings travels north from Templeton through various New Hampshire towns to the Acworth church in 1821, and finally to Newport in 1822. The relationship is clear, even in this, the northernmost of the group. It is the only one built of brick and the style of the brick exterior is very similar to that of the church built at Deerfield two years later. The Deerfield steeple is dramatically different, however, and it is the steeple which identifies the Newport church as falling most clearly into the Templeton group. The Newport steeple rises above the tower in three stages, a square, open-arched belfry below and two octagonal stages above, the top one having elliptical windows which match the window in the porch pediment. The spire atop the third stage has changed during its northern migration. The tall one at Templeton has been replaced by a small, foreshortened one at Newport. The Newport spire is a duplicate of its most recent predecessor in the run, at Acworth. (It is interesting that the steeple added in Jaffrey in 1823, the last in Peter Benes's discussion of the run, has a spire which compromises between the tall one at Templeton and the short one at Newport.) The portico at Templeton has become an enclosed porch at Newport. Though there are three porch entries, they are not connected by a common lintel as they are in Templeton, Fitzwilliam and Hancock. Again, in this respect the Newport church resembles its Acworth neighbor. The use of brick, which makes the Newport building so dramatically different, may have been urged by James Breck, as it is known that his business buildings were built of brick. The result is handsome. The indented arches in the porch and around the building with the interstices near the top give the church a graceful appearance. The 1887 *Manual of the Congregational Church in Newport, New Hampshire* states that John Leach built the church and that the "churches at Acworth, Croydon Four Corners, and other places were built after the same plans."

With few exceptions, such as the later nineteenth-century pews in the gallery, the earlier aspects of the interior have been lost to a twentieth-century redecoration. The 1887 *Manual* provides a good description of the early interior, and of the building's dedication in 1823:

> The interior, especially the high pulpit, was elaborately finished. Specimens of the columns are in the possession of Francis Boardman. The desk projected in such a way as to leave a recess underneath large enough for several persons to sit in. The pulpit was entered through this recess by stairs in the rear. The wall pews were square, and the rest parallelogram in shape, but very wide, affording end seats. The hinges, for the most part, sounding board and deacons' seats were dispensed with. There was a bell in the tower from the first . . . In the N.H. Patriot for March 10, 1823, appeared the following paragraph: "The new brick meetinghouse erected by the Congregational Society in Newport the Last season, will be dedicated to the service of ALMIGHTY GOD on Thursday, the 13th inst. It is expected a discourse will be delivered on the occasion by President Tyler, of Hanover." People came from all parts of the country to attend the exercises, so that the house was literally packed.

FIRST CHURCH

Deerfield, Massachusetts 1824

Finding new superlatives for Deerfield is difficult. All is very pastoral now on Old Deerfield's famous street, but this belies a tumultuous and trying past. There are reminders everywhere, in the earliest of the houses and particularly in the graveyard, that for more than fifty years the settlement was a frontier outpost, and the name of Bloody Brook in South Deerfield is not an alliterative coincidence. More than any other place in New England, Deerfield provides a poignant reminder of the inevitable clash between Indians and Europeans and also the colonial struggle of European powers, the English in New England and the French in Canada.

187 The fine simple interior viewed from the gallery.

188 The interior from the pulpit.

190 The meetinghouse in winter, showing the post office beside it.

The earliest settlement was in the late 1660s, and the present parish dates back to the gathering of the first congregation in 1673. The first meetinghouse was probably built about 1675, but was destroyed by an Indian attack. Both this and the building which replaced it were probably garrison-type buildings. In 1694, the settlers decided to build a larger house and the present post office at Deerfield, which stands just north of First Church, or Brick Church, is modeled after a drawing of the 1694 building. This was a square, hip-roofed meetinghouse with a central belfry. It must have been the building which stood within the garrison when the famous Indian attack of 1704 occurred. The congregation's pastor, John Williams, and more than a hundred other townspeople, were taken to Canada in captivity.

Though Deerfield remained a town on the edge of the frontier after the captives returned in 1706, the situation gradually began to stabilize. The peace agreed with the Iroquois in 1735 was an important factor. Deerfield became an important supply depot during the French and Indian War of the 1740s and 1750s. Indian attacks continued intermittently, with the last one recorded occurring in 1746. The increased security of the town probably played a large part in the decision to build Deerfield's fourth meetinghouse, in 1729. It was an oblong type, with a side entry and a tower which may have been added later. By the 1820s Deerfield's life had changed dramatically. After the Revolution the town turned back energetically to agricultural pursuits, and improved communication along the Connecticut

189 The façade of the meetinghouse.

River eventually made markets as far away as New York available for selling local livestock and other produce. In 1824, Deerfield voted to build a new meetinghouse, more in keeping with contemporary tastes, having determined the previous year that repairing the 1729 house was impractical. The project was not to cost more than $6000.

For a master builder they turned to Captain Winthrop Clapp of nearby Montague, Massachusetts. Deerfield is in every way a Connecticut River town, and it is logical that Clapp would draw his design from existing towns up and down the valley. The meetinghouse he built is definitely derivative of Damon's designs. It has even been suggested that Clapp may have worked for Damon at some point. The one Damon building represented in this book is the meetinghouse at Springfield, Massachusetts, and it is almost certain that Clapp had seen it. He must have been very familiar with Damon's Greenfield meetinghouse which is said to have resembled the Deerfield one closely, and stood only a few miles away. The body of the Deerfield meetinghouse is very similar to the house dedicated at Newport, New Hampshire, the year before, though it is unlikely that there was any direct influence involved. It is possible that the Greenfield building influenced both.

As at Newport, one finds intersticed arched brickwork all around the Deerfield meetinghouse, and the façade is also strikingly similar. The Deerfield porch has three entries. The central one is slightly taller and wider, with double-hung windows above. The similarities end as one glances upward. The elliptical window in the pediment, so typical of the Templeton group to which the Newport meetinghouse belongs, is lacking at Deerfield, as are the dentiled cornices. The steeple is the key difference. Clapp's steeple at Deerfield is undoubtedly a Damon steeple, not an ornate one inspired by Elias Carter as in the Templeton group. The tower at Deerfield is simply treated, with louvered arched windows and simple architraves. The steeple has the classic blind octagonal stages so typical of Damon, sparsely decorated with engaged columns on the first, and largest, stage.

The interior of the Deerfield meetinghouse has one truly outstanding feature: the pulpit is still in the tower end of the audience room. Though this design was far from rare in New England's early church-plan meetinghouses, there are very few examples where it was not altered later by placing the pulpit at the far end of the long axis. The rest of the interior has seen various changes, including the readjustment of the arrangement of the box pews, as well as a wide variety of painting and frescoing on the walls. This painting has even included stars on the ceiling and a rising sun in the pulpit recess. The present, muted color scheme leaves one free to enjoy the uncluttered grace of the curved gallery and domed ceiling.

It is fitting that Old Deerfield's street should have a meetinghouse as fine as this brick building. The Deerfield cemetery, down Albany Road behind both the meetinghouse and Deerfield Academy, is unquestionably one of New England's most important. The stones date from the late seventeenth century, and there are numerous examples of fine carving. It also contains the common grave of the forty-eight victims of the 1704 attack and the stone of their pastor, John Williams. There is also the stone of Lt. Mehuman Hinsdell, who died in 1736, aged sixty-three. The stone proclaims him "the first male child born in this place, and was twice captivated by the Indian salvages [*sic*]."

FIRST
CONGREGATIONAL CHURCH

Cheshire, Connecticut 1826

The story of the creation of new parishes, and eventually new towns, due to the geography and politics of a region should, by now, be fairly familiar. Just as Avon is a direct descendant of the original Hartford settlement, via Farmington, so Cheshire is a direct descendant of New Haven, via Wallingford. Wallingford was settled in 1669. Initially men went out to the western meadows to farm by day and returned by night. Gradually they became bolder and a small settlement called West Farms sprang up. It was this small cluster of houses which eventually became Cheshire. The process followed the usual pattern; as the settlement grew, the settlers grew tired of traveling to meeting at Wallingford and once again a river divided the two groups. In 1718 the westerners petitioned the Connecticut General

191 A 19th-century treatment of the pulpit wall.

Assembly to form a new parish. At first it was refused. In 1722, the town of Wallingford voted the settlers the right to call a minister for the winter months, but this only increased the West Farmers' desire for their own, permanent church. Though the parent town had resisted on the basis that it "did not seem best to spoil a town to make a village," the West Farms request was granted in the spring of 1723 and they gathered their own church.

The first meetinghouse was a rude one indeed, measuring 40 by 30 feet, with no belfry or turret, one entry, and benches within. There is no mention of a gallery. Clearly the congregation saw it as woefully inadequate, and in 1737 they began to build a new one. This was an oblong clapboarded house with a side entrance. The tower at the north end, which was not added until 1790, had an open arched belfry topped by a spire. In its final form this Cheshire meetinghouse was similar to the one built by the First Church at Hartford in 1738 and 1739. The new Cheshire meetinghouse stood on the town green, with its main eastern entrance toward the turnpike (now route 10) which comes from the south and runs north toward Farmington. The present church is built behind the site of the second one and looks over the green toward the main road.

The congregation's years in the second meetinghouse were dominated by the pastorate of John Foote, who served the community from 1767 till 1813, another typical early New England "till death do us part" ministerial arrangement. Though most of Foote's ministry was

192 The interior: note the high domed ceiling.

193 The meetinghouse overlooking the town green.

194 The door leading from the audience room to the vestibule.

195 A detail of the gallery railing. Note the decorative rim around the ceiling dome above.

successful, in 1778 he became the subject of a most interesting controversy. A group of unhappy church members demanded a meeting of the Congregational Consociation of New Haven County to review Foote's performance. These Consociations had been established in the Saybrook Platform of 1708 to address all manner of theologically related cases with representatives of all the congregations in the area present. The accusations against Foote included

> Mr Foote prayed with his eyes open; a friend of one of the aggrieved brethren
> called on Mr Foote and he did not even offer him a glass of cider; stating in a
> sermon that Adam built the ark; Pharaoh, that haughty monarch, beheaded John
> the Baptist; partiality in catechising children of different families; presenting a gift
> sent by another person by request as though it were his own gift.

Foote survived with an admonition, though it seemed clear enough that he had to be more careful with his biblical references.

As the Cheshire church turned one hundred, the congregation was considering a new meetinghouse. The one where John Foote had preached so adroitly was in need of major repairs and was out of fashion. The town voted a tax of thirty-six cents on every dollar to be paid in three installments, one in 1825, and one in each of the two following years. The same

1825 meeting when the tax was imposed also saw agreement on siting the new house at the town green. In early 1826 the steeple on the old meetinghouse was taken down. Its timber, and later other materials from the old house, was used in constructing the new one. By December 1826 the congregation was meeting in the "basement room" of the new meetinghouse. In 1827, the new house was completed and the old one came down, dramatically changing the appearance of Cheshire's town center.

Cheshire's third and present meetinghouse, like the ones at Warren and Avon, falls into a group of early nineteenth-century Connecticut meetinghouses with graceful two-staged steeples topped by tall spires. The designs at Warren and Avon are somewhat similar; but at Cheshire, built about nine years later, the style had evolved. The pilastered porch at Warren and Avon has become a pedimented entrance bay with a shallow, but impressive, portico. The layout of the entry doors is similar to that at both the other buildings, but the moldings here are somewhat bolder. The dentiled cornice of the pediment mirrors that of the roof. What makes this façade so imposing, however, is the use of stop-fluted Ionic columns and the shadow pilasters which mirror the columns' carving. The only element which detracts from the striking effect is the odd placement of a double-hung window in the middle of the pediment face. Kelly provides the likely suggestion that this was a later addition. Though the form of the steeple at Cheshire is similar to Avon, it is again somewhat grander. The tower has a clock on the front and lunette windows on the sides. The steeple rises in two stages, both of which are octagonal. The first is an open belfry supported by Ionic columns; the second is solid, with arched louvers alternating with patterned panels. Both stages are topped by delicate Chippendale balustrades while the tower is topped by a simpler version. The spire is a ribbed and shingled one similar to, though slightly larger than, the one at Avon.

Though the interior has undergone some changes, the detail is outstanding. The rim around the fine domed ceiling is reminiscent of the one at United Church at New Haven. The galleries are supported by fluted Ionic columns and the gallery rails have dentiling and fine decorative carving. The original high pulpit stood at the other end of the audience room but, as with most meetinghouses so oriented, this was later changed. In 1857, the building was severely damaged by lightning which passed through the main part of the structure. When the building was restored the floor was relaid, the pulpit was lowered and its position reversed. The present curved slip pews may have been installed at this time, though there is a reference in the seating plan of 1827 which suggests "that the most advanced of life should occupy the seats nearest the pulpit in front circular slips."

Though this fine Cheshire meetinghouse falls into the same stylistic period as Warren and Avon, it is more specifically related to the meetinghouses at Milford (1823), Southington (1828) and particularly Litchfield (1829). At Cheshire, as with a number of the others, Hoadley is often suggested as the designer. Certain structural themes have been adduced in support of the claim, but there is no documentary evidence for it. Hoadley was certainly not the principal builder in this case, as the church records clearly state that the joinery and carpentry were performed by Hall & Winton, who received $2150 for their labors, about a quarter of the building cost.

FIRST PARISH CHURCH

Quincy, Massachusetts 1827

By 1820, New England's architectural landscape was on the brink of dramatic evolution. The world of Charles Bulfinch, Peter Banner, Samuel McIntire and Asher Benjamin was about to be supplanted by the Greek Revival. McIntire died in 1811. Bulfinch moved to Washington in 1820 to take over the completion of the Capitol. Benjamin, who lived till 1845, was seeing his design-book through multiple editions and incarnations. Elias Carter was in Mendon, Massachusetts, finishing a church not radically different from the one he built at Templeton nine years earlier. Later, the perambulating Carter settled down near his birthplace, in Worcester. He made a successful transition to the Greek Revival style but he stayed in Worcester. It was left to representatives of the new generation to fill the void left by the first great American professional architects in Boston. The leading lights of the Greek Revival were Isaiah Rogers, Solomon Willard and Alexander Parris. It was Parris who designed the new building for the Adams family church in Quincy.

Parris is a good example of what the new professionalism in America's architecture meant to individuals. He was born in Hebron, Maine, in 1780 and trained as a carpenter's apprentice, at which he must have shown promise. One hundred, or even fifty, years before this might have either led to a successful career as an itinerant joiner or master builder, or to being told by his father to consider more serious pursuits than design. As the eighteenth century turned, however, it meant the opportunity for Parris to go to Portland and study. He designed a number of fine houses there, three of which still stand. He later served as a Captain in the War of 1812, settling in Boston afterwards. In 1818, he was listed in the Boston City Directory as "Architect and Engineer."

His years in Boston were productive. He built many houses on Beacon Hill, St Paul's Church (with Solomon Willard) (1819) and Quincy Market near Fanueil Hall (1825). Both Willard and Parris were protégés of Bulfinch's, and Parris served as superintendant of Bulfinch's Massachusetts General Hospital (1819), the master's last Boston commission. Parris later served as civil engineer at the Portsmouth, New Hampshire, navy yard. He died in his ancestral town of Pembroke, Massachusetts, in 1852. If it is possible to envy someone his obituaries, then one might envy Parris his. Here are excerpts from two, though we can be sure the first allows some hyperbole:

> To no other person do so large a number of imposing and substantial buildings
> which characterize our city, owe their distinction.
>
> (*Boston Herald*)

196 The façade at Quincy from across the burial ground.

> Eminently endowed by nature with a commanding intellect and a refined taste, he added to them on all occasions an urbanity of manner and integrity of purpose which made him respected in society and esteemed in business. He was too honest and generous to be wealthy . . . and he never had an enemy.
>
> (Boston Traveler)

Parris's most famous building outside Boston is the Unitarian church in Quincy.

John Adams felt that the Bible contained "the most perfect philosophy, the most perfect morality, and the most refined policy;" in fact, in the light of the Commandments, it was "the most Republican book in the World." He also felt that religion was the only thing which "preserved the Adamses in all their ramifications, in such numbers, health, peace, comfort and mediocrity . . . without which they would have been rakes, fops, sots, gamblers, starved with hunger, frozen with cold, scalped by Indians, etc., etc., etc., been melted away and disappeared." This certainly must have been a factor in the generosity of his contributions toward the construction of the new parish building at Quincy, contributions which included Quincy granite. John, John Quincy and both their wives are interred in "The Stone Temple's" crypt.

The Quincy church is one of the best early examples of Greek Revival architecture in America, a stylistic development typified by massive designs, colonnaded porticos and classic lines. Everywhere, porticos were incorporated in new designs or oddly appended to existing structures. The execution of Parris's plans began in 1829, but the building was not dedicated until late 1828. The construction was a herculean project. The entire exterior is of Quincy granite. Charles Francis Adams described the moving of one of the portico columns in his diary in June 1828:

> After some conversation and taking tea, we returned to town over Milton Hill and met the last of the heavy stone Columns for the Meeting House. It was dragged by thirty five yoke of oxen and was a tolerable load.

Young Charles Francis was also at the dedication a few months later and was disarmingly unimpressed:

> The object I had in view was to attend the dedication of the New Church in Quincy, to plant the acorns my father gave to my charge, and to obtain the things which I had left in my Summer's residence here. The day cleared off bitterly cold before the services were finished. They were not at all of an impressive character to my mind, but I differ so much from others in these feelings that my tastes are to me troubles.

The centerpiece of the exterior is the pedimented portico which rests on four massive Doric pillars. The portico contains all three entries, and the entry bay rises behind it, with the tower and cupola above the bay. Six columns support the simply decorated tower dome, and the tower arrangement does bear some similarity in basic form to Bulfinch's First Church at

197 The coffered ceiling, showing a previous painting treatment.

198 The interior with its exquisite domed ceiling.

Lancaster, Massachusetts. But there is little or no adornment on the exterior of the building. Simple cornices are used throughout with three single round-headed windows on each side of the main body of the church, which extends with a pitched roof behind the entrance bay. The clock in the tower does not break the mood very consciously created here. The building is a monument to permanence, and its massiveness is its message.

The interior is overwhelming in a different way. The domed ceiling is of remarkable proportions and style and extends almost the entire width of the building. It has been painted in various ways but is now monochrome. It is unusually coffered, with three rings of indentations. The outer ring's coffers contain rosettes, the next and largest are blank, while the inner, and smallest, ring repeats the rosettes. The center medallion is surrounded by a key-pattern ring. The rest of the interior is excellent with finely carved and sparsely supported galleries, but from any angle it is the magnificent ceiling which dominates.

It seems appropriate to conclude with this Quincy church, as it represents such a radical departure from its predecessors. Puritan simplicity in wood or even brick, still evident in the Cheshire meetinghouse built two years before, has been dramatically altered at Quincy. This massive building with its startlingly new design stands at the brink of a new age. The delicate grace of the earlier buildings has been replaced by the impressive, monumental but quintessentially nineteenth-century quality of this granite temple.

199 The Adams' crypt.

Notes and Acknowledgments

First and foremost let me thank Abbott Lowell Cummings of Yale whose careful assistance and sensible approach kept me from falling into many a trap. From the façade gables at Hingham to the complicated question of David Hoadley he was always available for help and consultation and served as a principal reader of the text. I have listed my other sources, literary and personal, by section. These lists, particularly as far as people are concerned, are always dangerous. Tim and I were universally well-received and assisted, and any omissions are a reflection of my forgetfulness rather than any failing on their part. This listing is not intended as a complete bibliography but rather is designed to cite those people and sources which were most helpful. I have rarely repeated references to general source material, most of which are cited under the Introduction. The most up-to-date and complete bibliography in this field can be found in Peter Benes and Philip D. Zimmerman, *New England Meeting House and Church: 1630–1850* (Boston 1979).

INTRODUCTION Numerous general sources were useful. Particular thanks go to the following: Sidney Ahlstrom's *A Religious History of the American People* (New Haven 1972) is not only the best book on American religious history, it is one of the best historical works I have ever encountered; Peter Benes and Philip D. Zimmerman, *New England Meeting House and Church: 1630–1850*, (Boston 1979); Daniel Boorstin, *The Colonial Experience* (New York 1958); Marian Card Donnelly, *The New England Meetinghouses of the Seventeenth Century* (Middletown, Conn. 1968); J. Frederick Kelly, *Early Connecticut Meetinghouses* (New York 1948); Frederick Merk, *History of the Westward Movement* (New York 1978); Harold W. Rose, *The Colonial Houses of Worship in America* (New York 1963); Charles E. Place, "From Meetinghouse to Church in New England," in Old-Time New England (OTNE), vols 13–14, 1923; Edmund Ware Sinnott, *Meetinghouse and Church in Early New England* (New York 1963), a useful index of pre-1830 buildings; Chard Powers Smith, *Yankees and God* (New York 1954), a quirky but intriguing book; William Warren Sweet, *The Story of Religion in America* (New York 1950), a worthy predecessor to Ahlstrom; Ola Elizabeth Winslow, *Meetinghouse Hill 1630–1783*, (New York 1952). The Bradford quotation is taken from an edition prior to Samuel Eliot Morison's update, for no particular reason other than that I thought it would be fun.

THE OLD SHIP, HINGHAM Thanks to the Rev. Kenneth La Fleur. Sources included Gladys Stark's *The Old Ship Meeting House*; G. Harris Danzberger's *Meeting House Meanderings* (1980); and John Coolidge's "Hingham Builds a Meetinghouse," in *New England Quarterly* 34, December 1961. Also Murray Corse's article in OTNE, July 1930.

FRIENDS MEETINGHOUSE, NEWPORT Thanks to Esther Fisher Benson for both her personal assistance and her pamphlet,

The Great Meeting House. Also to Antoinette Downing for her excellent article on the meetinghouse in *Newport History*, 132, Fall 1968.

ST PAUL'S, WICKFORD We received most gracious on-site assistance in Wickford and were provided with a copy of Hunter C. White's *Old St Paul's in Narragansett* (1957).

WEST PARISH MEETINGHOUSE, WEST BARNSTABLE Many thanks to William Soller for his kind assistance with archives. He provided much information including the helpful monograph by Walter Goehring on the history of the parish (1959). Edwin Goodell's article in OTNE, July 1930, was very useful.

CHRIST CHURCH, BOSTON Thanks to the Rev. Russell Way, associate vicar, and to Al, for their patience. Suzanne Foley's article in OTNE, Jan.–Mar. 1961, was very useful.

TRINITY CHURCH, NEWPORT Particular thanks to the Rev. Marsden Price for his thoughtful advice and the loan of his copy of Norman Isham's *Trinity Church in Newport* (1936).

OLD SOUTH MEETINGHOUSE, BOSTON Many thanks to Cynthia Stone and staff. Most information was drawn from nineteenth-century histories, the most important being Hamilton Hill's two-volume *History of the Old South Church* (1890).

KING'S CHAPEL, BOSTON Thanks to the Rev. Carl Scovel and staff. Particularly useful for background was André Mayer's monograph, *King's Chapel. The First Century* (1976). Also Sidney F. Kimball's article, "The Colonial Amateurs and their Models: Peter Harrison," in *Architecture* 53, 1926.

TOURO SYNAGOGUE, NEWPORT Particular thanks to Rabbi Dr Theodore Lewis for both his direct assistance and his history in the *Bulletin of the Newport Historical Society*, Summer 1975.

OLD TRINITY CHURCH, BROOKLYN Thanks to the Rev. R. J. Glaude, rector of the new Trinity Church.

FIRST CHURCH OF CHRIST, FARMINGTON Thanks to the Rev. Richard W. Bauer for his assistance and patience. Many general sources include J. Frederick Kelly's *Early Connecticut Meetinghouses*, op. cit., and Lydia Hewes's *A Short History of Farmington* (1935).

THREE MAINE MEETINGHOUSES Thanks to the German Protestant Society at Waldoboro, to Mabel Longe at the Old Walpole Meetinghouse Association, and to Clifton Walker at Alna.

UNION CHURCH AND OLD ST MARY'S, WEST CLAREMONT Thanks to the Rev. Ronald Prinn at Union and Mr Jusley at St Mary's who provided me with Hector LaMontagne's monograph on that parish's history.

FIRST BAPTIST CHURCH, PROVIDENCE Thanks to all the staff who were so helpful and provided me with two monographs, the second a parish history by Marguerite Appleton (1975). Also Norman Isham's history (1925).

OLD MEETINGHOUSE, ROCKINGHAM Thanks to town manager Lawrence McAuliffe and to GRM. Sources include John Williams's *The Redeemed Captive* (Amherst, Mass. 1976); Lyman S. Hayes's *History of Rockingham* (1907) and *Old Rockingham Meeting House* (1915); Herbert W. Congden's *Old Vermont Houses* (1946) and G. F. Webb's *Rockingham Historical Notes* (1969).

SABBATHDAY LAKE SHAKER MEETINGHOUSE Thanks to Brother Theodore Johnson. I made use of Sister R. Mildred Barker's *The Sabbathday Lake Shakers* (1978).

FIRST RELIGIOUS SOCIETY, NEWBURYPORT Thanks to the Rev. Steeves, particularly for leading me to Minnie Atkinson's *A History of the First Religious Society in Newburyport* (1933).

CHURCH ON THE HILL, LENOX Thanks to the Rev. Kyte for his careful attention. Sources include the monograph published by the church on the parish history and Peter Benes's "The Templeton 'Run'" in OTNE, 68, Winter-Spring 1978, and R. DeWitt Mallary's *Lenox and the Berkshire Highlands* (1902).

THE OLD FIRST CHURCH, OLD BENNINGTON Many thanks to the Allens (particularly for their advice on speeding tickets!) and to GRM. Also Abbott Cummings for his recollections. Sources include Isaac Jennings's *The One Hundred Year Old Meetinghouse* (1907); Dr L. Ravi-Booth's *Dedication of the Restored Old First Church* (1937); Lawrence Woodhouse's article on Lavius Fillmore in *Vermont History*, Autumn 1969; and H. W. Congdon's article in the same journal, June 1959, and his book *Old Vermont Houses* (1956).

THOMAS HOOKER'S HARTFORD DESCENDANTS Thanks to the Revs. McLean and Elmore and their staffs. Sources include Roland H. Bainton's *Thomas Hooker and the Puritan Contribution to Democracy* (1958), R. H. Potter's *Hartford's First Church* (1932), Mary James's National Register Application for Second (South) Church, and Kelly, *op. cit.*

FIRST CHURCH, TEMPLETON Thanks to the Rev. Ruth Martin and family for their personal attention, and to Benes's "The Templeton 'Run'", *op. cit.*

OLD ROUND CHURCH, RICHMOND Many thanks to the Riggses, particularly to Harriet for her time and her article on the community and the church's restoration in the Spring 1980 issue of *Vermont Life*. Also to David Ruell for his fine article in *Historical New Hampshire*, Summer/Fall 1981, which traces the architectural lineage of "The 'Round' Meetinghouses of New Hampshire and Vermont".

THE NEW HAVEN GREEN Thanks to the Rev. John Hay of United Church and to Dr Peter Ives of Center Church for their assistance and general materials provided. Also Kelly, *op. cit.* and once more Abbott Cummings.

FIRST CHURCH OF CHRIST, LANCASTER Many thanks to the Rev. Thomas Wintle for his assistance and company and for providing me with Alexander St-Ivanyi's monograph (1972). I also consulted Harold Kirker's *The Architecture of Charles Bulfinch* (1969).

CONGREGATIONAL CHURCH, WARREN Thanks to the Rev. Peter Marsden for his direction and assistance. Sources include Kelly, *op. cit.*, and Lucy Sackett Curtiss's *Warren Congregational Church* (1956). My thanks also to the staff of the Town Clerk's office.

CONGREGATIONAL CHURCH, AVON Thanks to the Rev. T. Schoonmaker. Sources include two parish histories, the second by Barbara R. Rettig. Also Kelly, *op. cit.*

FIRST CHURCH, SPRINGFIELD Thanks to the Rev. James Douglas Riddle and to Francis Potter's parish history.

SOUTH CONGREGATIONAL CHURCH, NEWPORT Thanks to the Rev. James Gray and to Howard Bennett. Sources include the *Manual of the Congregational Church in Newport, N.H.*, published by the parish in 1887, and Samuel H. Edes' *History* (1954).

FIRST CHURCH, DEERFIELD Thanks to Donald Friary, and also to the Rev. and Mrs Ronald T. Evans.

FIRST CONGREGATIONAL CHURCH, CHESHIRE Thanks to the Rev. Wayne Sandau and his staff. Sources include Edward Gumprecht's parish history (1974), and Kelly, *op. cit.*

FIRST PARISH CHURCH, QUINCY Many thanks to Owen Della Lucca, gracious archivist at the First Parish Church.

Further and more general thanks go first to Tim Imrie. His photographs are excellent, particularly when one considers the difficulty in shooting church interiors, something we tried to stress more than previous books of this type have done. In addition to Tim's technical skills, his affable attitude and good company made our many days on the road together happy rather than tedious. Secondly, my usual thanks to Lindy Whiton whose generous hospitality to both of us made this book possible; also my usual thanks to Cathy's magic fingers. In London my thanks go to all the Neville-Rolfes and their spouses for ceaseless hospitality. I was blessed with many editors: on that front my thanks go to Sue and Larry and (much to their disbelief) Alex and Charles. Many thanks to my own family for assistance ranging from advice on religious history from my ministerial papa and learned mother to the library and graceful assistance of GRM. Also thanks to Jay, Mimi, Colin, Myrtle, Earl, Stephen and, lastly, to the ever-patient Frances.

Index

Numbers in *italics* refer to illustrations